THINKING ABOUT LITERACY

Young children and their language

Fred Sedgwick

London and New York

First published 1999
by Routledge
11 New Fetter Lane, London EC4P 4EE

Simultaneously published in the USA and Canada
by Routledge
29 West 35th Street, New York, NY 10001

Typeset in Garamond 3 by
Keystroke, Jacaranda Lodge, Wolverhampton
Printed and bound in Great Britain by
Page Bros (Norwich) Ltd

British Library Cataloguing in Publication Data
A catalogue record for this book is available from the British Library

Library of Congress Cataloging in Publication Data
Sedgwick, Fred.
Thinking about literacy : young children and their language / Fred Sedgwick.
p.   cm.
Includes bibliographical references (p.   ) and index.
1. Children—Language. 2. Language acquisition. 3. Children—
Books and reading. I. Title.
LB1139.L3S34 1999
401'.93—dc21   98–25910
CIP

ISBN 0–415–16865–1

In the beginning was the word
                    St John 1:1

Only one thing remained secure against all losses – language
                                                    Paul Célan

   Not in entire forgetfulness,
   And not in utter nakedness,
But trailing clouds of glory do we come . . .
                                        Wordsworth

CONTENTS

CONTENTS

ACKNOWLEDGEMENTS

Individuals and schools who helped with parts of this book.

Dawn Sedgwick, Helen Arnold, Liz Waterland, Cindy, Duncan and Alastair Bathgate, Brian Hatton, Lucinda Symons, Margaret Browne, Stephanie Lacey, Jacquie, Simon and James Knott, Revd Colin Sedgwick, Revd Peter Townley, John Cotton, the Toft family and (as always) Father Henry Burns Elliot.

Parkgate Infants, Watford; Tacolneston First, Norfolk; Tattingstone Primary, Ipswich; Raeburn Infants, Ipswich; Clifford Road Primary, Ipswich; Icknield Walk First, Royston, Hertfordshire; Oxhey Infants, Bushey, Hertfordshire; St Lawrence's Roman Catholic Voluntary Aided Primary, Cambridge; St Nicholas Church of England Voluntary Aided Primary, Stevenage; Peartree Way Nursery, Stevenage; Fairfields Primary, Cheshunt; Boxford Primary, Suffolk.

Thank you to Sarah Fisher for her poem 'Departure'.

Thanks also to *Montessori Education*, in which some paragraphs have appeared before.

DEDICATORY POEM

To the Children

The Children leave the building
Alex and Katrina
Adam Unbenham and Shazadan
Alison Greengown and Gopal

The Children leave the building

autumn leaf and leaf and leaf
and smell of burning in the air
and scarlet roses and scarlet roses
and the one silver birch left
and Ford and Citroen and Renault
and Opel and Volvo and Vauxhall

The Children leave the building

There is no dance and no drama
no painting no poem no page of sums
no songs to sing no construction to be constructed
and checked and measured and drawn

or drawn and measured and checked
and constructed

There is no debate no instrumental playing

There is no art no science no religion

The Children leave the building

and Simone and Ravinder and Kim Pan
and Syreeta and the other Simone and James
and Gareth and Alan and Margaret and Jane
and Sharif and Surinder and Melanie and Mark

and I sit and play the piano
and I sit and paint

and yawn

Rose and bulb and rose
and bulb and rose and
bulb

and autumn leaves

(Sedgwick 1991)

Introduction

LANGUAGE AND HUMANITY

Literacy hour or literacy life?

'Why did God call me Joanna?'
(six-year-old girl)

'Language and humanity'. These are imposing words, I know. They are 'impressive because of size, bearing, dignity or grandeur', as the *Longman Concise English Dictionary* defines 'imposing'. But the root of 'impose' is the Latin word meaning, among other things, to 'inflict, set over, lay as a burden' (*Shorter Oxford English Dictionary*). Whether because of their 'grandeur' or not, the words *impose* on you, the reader, in a literal sense. Their abstractness, or their vagueness, one might say, lays a burden on you.

Well, I feel the same. Abstractions like 'language', 'humanity', 'truth' or 'beauty' force a reaction in which we dismiss, irritated, whatever is being introduced. Language and *what*? *What* and humanity? I once heard a teacher dismiss an earlier book of mine with the remark 'it's a bit meaning-of-life-for me'. In the same spirit, I prefer poems with concrete nouns in them – dog, lamp-post, beer. With abstract nouns, I suspect someone is trying to slip something past me by sleight of tongue.

But I have two defences to a possible charge of pretentiousness. The first is that learners will speak and write throughout this book, justifying my words, and making it as practical as it is possible for a book about education to be. This book is, like Eliot's garden, full of leaves that are in turn full of the voices of children. And the children's speeches and writing are full of important words. A sample:

Why do you get older when it's your birthday?
Why have people got names?
How do people talk?
How does the sun light up?
How does the river move?
Why are beaches by the sea?
Why are there millions of stones by the beach?

These are five year olds. These and their other questions are discussed on pp. 45–7. These children are slightly older:

1

How did God come into the world without getting born?
What does God look like?
Is Jesus bald?
How was the first man born when there was no one to have a baby?
How do we know if a man is horrible or not?

And then, after all this big talk about the serious issues of our times (and all times): 'How do you make salad cream?' and 'Why do aliens have longer half terms than we do?' and 'Why is it, when I am sick, there's always carrots?' There is more about these children in Chapter 3, as I move away from my task of imposing burdens, towards the more important task of concentrating on the voices of children. It is enough to say here that a girl I was teaching once asked the question 'When will I die?' The reader might guess that none of these questions was asked during the literacy hour.

The second defence is this: the imposition of my words (language and humanity) is justified even without those children and their eloquence. Language, like nothing else, encapsulates our humanity and the possibility of our humanity's survival. Tell me how you feel about your mother or father or brother or sister or wife or husband or son or daughter – but do it without speaking or writing.

You can, of course, draw, dance or act. Indeed, all of the other arts have a more primal claim on our humanity and its responses, and they can be more subtle and powerful in some tasks considered, pre-eminently, language's tasks. They can persuade and cajole. I have argued their case elsewhere (Sedgwick 1993). But their power stems from the fact that they are, primarily, arts: artificial creations. Although language often constitutes an art, too, and although we make self-conscious things of it, poems, dramas and novels, it is also a root, deep under our primary means of communication, from which our most crude and our most subtle remarks bloom. Those parts of conversations on the telephone and in the office, in the living room and over the dining table stem from something that is, essentially, what makes us human. And then it is there in those poems that we all write, if only in our minds, and if we are brave enough, that are like (if we are unlucky) frail petals and (if we are lucky and chosen and gifted and industrious) like the toughest blooms imaginable.

So art, dance and drama may have come first in time. Once we daubed and carved, moved and acted. But language has always had an underlying function. If we cannot use words we are seriously disabled. Indeed, we need language to talk about the other arts. Imagine dance or drama without talk: if not during them, before them and after them. We need language to order food, to express needs and to love. Because we must use language to express our desires, negotiate our position, formulate our emotions, it is through language that we can understand, or comprehend, our humanity. Through language we communicate in a unique way. In dance or drama, in paint or sculpture, there is an admitted gauzy mist. What do they mean by that? How can we understand this? With language, the same gauze is there – but we behave as if it isn't. We behave as if a certain clarity is possible, as if words mean exactly what they say, as if my words mean exactly the same to you as they do to me. *Just say what you mean*, we say. *Tell it to my face.* Mincing paints, or brushstrokes, or dance steps or the notes on a stave or in a chord might be a creative possibility. Mincing words, though, is to prevaricate.

The human species has been rightly defined as 'the animal that talks': other beasts relate with each other in terms of sounds and bodily movements, but their systems are extremely narrow when compared to the complexity of even a human baby's communication. Indeed, human life is hard to conceive without the benefit of language: try to imagine a wordless school, or wordless love, or wordless politics. The power of naming is still there in the taboos, religious and sexual, associated with certain beings or things. Even more explicitly, religion links language with humanity when St John links the Creator with the Word (*logos*) in St John 1:1.

Other religious texts show understanding of this humanity–language connection. Whether we are believers or not we face, in talking or writing about language, an issue of primal importance. Adam does something essentially human as he names the creatures that God has provided in the world (Genesis 2:19–20). Adam was given the Arabic script by God. Indra invented speech, and Odin was credited with the invention of the runic alphabet. And, following Adam, Indra and Odin, many humans have felt that the ability to control follows the ability to name. Socrates speaks of the gods as those responsible for naming things properly (Plato: Cratylus). And in modern times it is the moment when the deaf and blind Helen Keller understands that things have names that her behaviour loses much of its wildness and becomes what we call human, as I try to show in this poem, written for children:

Helen Keller and the Pump

My hands pulled back
from the furious shock
of water's mute
splash on forearms, fingers.

Annie hammered
WATER twenty times on
my amazed palm
and words broke in at last.

I rush round the
garden: GROUND, PUMP, GRASS, TREE.
Name it! Name it!
She drummed on my palm words

for a gargling
snarling blind Eve, to set
her free, running
in the garden, naming.
(Sedgwick 1994)

So we can see that language has enormous significance for us all as humans in its role, if not of *making* us human, at least helping us to articulate and celebrate our humanity, and also in enabling us to face up to its realities.

But when humanity's reality is tested in ultimate ways language assumes an even greater importance. 'Only one thing remained secure against all losses – language,' said the poet Paul Célan in a radio broadcast. As a Jew, he would have understood the importance of language in the context of the horrors of the Holocaust. When the possibility of a jackboot in the face of the innocent potentially is present at every waking or sleeping moment of every day (this was how it felt to at least one survivor of the Holocaust: see Speigelman 1987), only the mind and its words are free. There is no art, no drama, no dance.

Centrality of language

The centrality of language is as valid in the smaller contexts of violence as it is in the imaginably larger ones. Here, for example, is a scene all teachers can imagine readily: a line of backs which, when urgently broken up, reveals two sweaty faces, four glowering eyes, glimpsed white knuckles, smells of mud and (later) the watching wonderment of bystanders sloping off, still absorbed (heads over shoulders) in the suddenly forbidden activity ('Just what is going on here?'). As teachers, parents, nursery nurses and classroom helpers (i.e., in all cases, as teachers) we have been there. We have all brought in by the wrists or the hands the wrestlers, the boxers, the frantic kickers, still wildly protesting their innocence. Some of us, indeed, have been those wrestlers, those boxers, those frantic kickers.

On the occasion I am describing, the teacher separates them, asking 'What's the problem?' And the children forget, for a moment, the substantive issue of the fight, and ask, brows furrowed: 'What's a problem?' From this conversation in this school, a way of thinking about violence emerged that involved, as Annabelle Dixon, the teacher who told me this story, put it, 'giving them the language'. Maybe it is not a question of teaching them to think, or giving them language (they have both already), but simply a matter of giving them words like 'problem', 'talk' and 'discuss'.

I asked a group of six year olds what are the central words that might show children ways round conflict; words that might show them what it is to be a human that can use words to solve moral problems. I said: 'You know you shouldn't fight? . . . that you should talk about the bad times when fighting seems the thing to do? . . . well, what words might you find useful, instead of the kicks and punches?' The teacher nominated three scribes who wrote down, in turns, what the other children offered. This is what they came up with:

Stop everybody lets be friends.
Stop fighting we will be in trouble.
Plese stop fighting someone will badly be heat [hurt].
We will be friends.
i'm sorry.
I'm going to tell the teacher.
Stop the violence
this is the last draw [straw].
lets stop the fight.
can we be qites [quits].
thats the end of the fight.
that done it.
I hert myself.
I know a better game than fighting lets be freind
calm don
leave me alone
stop or you will get a black
shace hands and be firends
stop or one of you will be in hospital
we will be firends
lets go and play another game
be calm don't be rogeh [rough]
this is silly
why are we doing this

We were collecting these comments at 3.00 in the afternoon, and one of the scribes wrote on the back of her sheet 'I am going home.' This is a use of language – for the sake of a truthful joke that might detonate only much later, when the joker has gone home – that is largely unrecognised by teachers among school children.

The remarks recorded are of several kinds: things heard from adults, things said in desperation, attempts at negotiation. Also, higher authority is referred to, either as a threat ('I'll tell . . .) or as a feared sanction. At some points – particularly in the last remark quoted – we see that existential desperation that we all feel at some terrible moments in our lives. These sayings give us a vivid glimpse at times and places on the playground which we usually don't see, except in our memories, and at the moments when the flashpoints bring us on to the scene as duty teachers.

Language is vatic. It is the poet-prophet of human life. A six-year-old girl writes 'does God blive in me?' and is, through the agency of that sentence,

5

able to muse (the pun on the words, 'amuse/the Muses' is significant) on an eternal problem. But she has reversed that problem with mind-jarring suddenness, using her language in a way few adults could. Much as a poet like Blake (or, in our own day, Geoffrey Hill) or a prophet like Amos have the roles of tellers of truths that grind against the fashionable contemporary grain, so language, under the disciplines of order and silence, of form and meditation, of shape and emotion, will move us forward; move, in particular, children forward against the contraries without which (Blake again) there is no progression.

I have tried to spell out the importance of language in order to contrast it with the fashionable political notions of the literacy hour, and of teaching literacy as if it could be separated from everything else; as if it weren't a prophet so much as a servant of the powerful in the cash nexus. Language teaches everything. As Rex Walford says in *The Times* of 17 December 1997

> The Government's announcement . . . that it is changing the rules of the game for primary schoolchildren to concentrate on literacy and numeracy . . . unaccountably ignores the creative possibility of using subjects such as geography, history, music and art as vehicles for literacy and numeracy.

I would go further. These other subjects are not just 'vehicles' for literacy and numeracy. They are bound up with them as surely as leaves, bark, trunk, roots, and sap are bound together.

Background to this book

This book is not an academic study, because I am not nor ever have been (slightly to my regret) an academic. The first essential part of my background, as far as my work for this book is concerned, was composed of thirty years working with students aged between four and eleven as, by turns, a class teacher, and a headteacher in three schools. Once my courage and my wife assured me I didn't need a contract any more, the second part began as I became a freelance writer on residential courses, at Arts festivals and similar events, an INSET (in-service training) provider in schools and groups of schools and (mostly) in schools working with children and older students. Much of my time in these jobs has been spent on helping children to read, talk and write with greater fluency and skill, and in thinking about these activities with practising teachers on courses, and with students preparing for the profession.

Looking back on those early years, when I still had a contract, I am appalled and embarrassed by the stupidity of some of what I did with children, and by the disrespect implicit in the ways I taught them. And my present work is as much an attempt at a reparation for some of my errors as much as it is a celebration of some of the successes children achieved alongside me. What were these errors? Here are some examples. I suspect that this list will give away in one paragraph much of the stance of this book:

- teaching as though children's writing at five or six years could usefully be copywriting under my own
- insisting that children wait in queues for spellings before they carried on with their writing
- assuming that a 'poem' could be written in one draft over three-quarters of an hour, even though my own attempts at poems at home were filling waste paper bins with screwed up abortions
- teaching children to read through the most banal of schemes instead of the kinds of materials that sprang naturally from engagements with the lives that the children were leading
- treating young children's marks – drawings, scribbles, early writing – without the kind of respect that would have made subsequent drawings, scribbles and writing much stronger
- allowing children to be 'assessed' by educational psychologists in tiny rooms, officially 'medical rooms' or the deputy's office, but really prison cells, separated from their friends, their classrooms, their families, their teachers, their worlds
- living a professional life as though my emotions and behaviour were in some way detached from those of the children I was teaching.

That will do. I wouldn't write that list were it not for three facts: first, that all teachers will recognise parts of it in their own practice; second, that some teachers still teach as though spelling and writing are synonymous, and, if they are different, spelling is more important than writing; and third, that some special needs teachers (really, they are pre-Warnock remedial teachers) still withdraw children from classrooms to take them to prison cells for questioning, even though the classroom's curriculum is now legally enforced. Thus they uncharitably and tactlessly emphasise what they, the child and the rest of the world already know the child can't do: bark at print. I can't dance. What would it be like if every day I was taken to a room with an effective and bossy dancer to have my every mistake minutely pointed out and analysed. For 'dancing' substitute some activity at which you see yourself as a failure.

Because I am not an academic, my interviews with children have been neither extensive nor systematic, as they are in books I admire, like Tizard and Hughes (1984) and Wells (1986). I am trying instead to show, through case studies of children I know in homes of friends of mine and in schools where there are teachers whom I respect, the power of what children learn through language: speech and writing. I hope that my examples show how much children can change in their use of language – some if it, no doubt, with our help as teachers; but also, much of it, through other agencies more mysterious: their intimate conversations with their friends, for example; their private thoughts; their imagination.

A note about thinking, talking and writing

The connections between thinking, which is private, and talking and writing, which are mostly public, need exploration. Some of us speak to ourselves, or write down our thoughts for our private consumption, and then find they've been overheard or read inadvertently. Part of our embarrassment stems from the fact that what we've said or written may be intensely private. But it also stems from the fact that, normally, both talking and writing are, to a greater or lesser extent, public. To have used them for private material is to be caught out. Talking and writing are, to take the matter further, different from each other. I can talk more quickly about these matters than I can possibly write about them, partly because I am conscious that my writing must have a greater form than my talking. The mechanical skills associated with writing, whether handwriting or typing, distract me from the content of my thought. Also, and more positively, in shaping my written words into whatever form I choose, or whatever emerges, I am changing my thoughts.

And the great advantage of writing over both thinking and talking is that I can go back to it and reflect on it as many times as I want. It is a commonplace that we can't take back something once it is said: our stupidities and tactlessnesses are in the public domain from the moment they're uttered, and we can just hope people forget about them. On the other hand, I have read and reread the pages of this book many times; I have revised on the screen as I wrote; I have printed many drafts, and scribbled all over them until they are unusable, and, in the light of my own revised thinking, and, occasionally, in the light of the suggestions of friends with similar passions about language and children to my own, I have revised again and again.

Some of the learning I referred to above is what we want children to learn. That is, after all, what schools are supposed to exist for. Much of that learning, though – more than we might like or guess – is what we'd rather they did not learn. For example, at almost every official moment of the school day, children learn about their lack of autonomy in the school. They are lined up to come in before lessons and after every break. They are dragooned in their dress. Often, they read what we as teachers tell them to read, rather than what they want to read. These sentences describe to me, as I reread them now, the situation one might expect in prison or, if that goes too far, the army.

When we look at the language that politicians, inspectors and advisers have used to discuss education and manipulate schools since the late 1980s, we note that seeing children as learners is less fashionable than it was once. Instead, children are seen as attaining or not; as progressing or not; as being 'on task' or 'off task'; as succeeding in, or failing, tests. The unobservable mental and affective processes going on inside the child's mind are of less concern than the apparatus of checklist and test, of league table. And one result of this is that we as teachers have learned, to a greater or lesser extent (depending, I suppose, on our vigilance) that watching our children is less important than watching our backs.

I want to suggest, in contrast, that it is in listening to and reading the words of children that we are doing our real job. We are then ourselves learners, and learners of what was always our professional concern: how children grow in an understanding of themselves, their world, and their relationship to that world. Some of this is what we want to learn. Some of it will delight us, some surprise us, or some even dismay us. Unfortunately, some of what we learn, we will deny, because it doesn't suit our current prejudices.

One prejudice is that children learn essentially and mostly from us as teachers. I will be writing later (pp. 29–34) about teachers who see the children they teach as having 'nil on entry'. But children, like Adam and Eve in their garden, are learners from the moment of their beginnings, years before their parents think of finding the right school for them. This is now so widely accepted, at least in theory (in practice we treat children still as blank pages) that it is quite difficult to sense what an odd idea it would have been to our parents and grandparents and (even, of course, more, the generations stretching back before them). They would have seen the young child surviving in order to learn; as preparing to live a life, rather than actually living it. The baby in the cradle was insignificant for generations. But, as Wells (1986:33) says, 'it has become clear from research over recent decades that the newborn baby is not as helpless as used to be supposed'.

Wordsworth, like the other Romantics (especially Rousseau and Coleridge) knew about the importance of childhood. The child is, in Wordsworth's words, 'father of the Man' and comes into the world 'trailing clouds of glory'. In some classrooms children are seen as ignoramuses who know nothing compared with us. Blank pages, empty pots, naughty humans, we write on them, fill them or correct them. On the other hand, if we take Wordsworth's poem ('Ode: Intimations of Mortality from Recollections of Early Childhood') seriously, we will treat children as knowing more than we do because, unless we are close to death, they know more than we do. They are closer to Heaven.

Thus the child is born with an impulse to make sense of the world and his or her experience of it. With that impulse in place, pulsing like a fontanelle from the beginning, learning becomes active more rapidly than is generally considered. Its growth has, indeed, largely outstripped our understanding of it, and our practice as teachers needs to improve in order to begin to understand it, and its serious implications for our practice. I have written with my wife (Sedgwick and Sedgwick 1996) about this growth, and demonstrated its pace and breadth: young babies survive, move, communicate and love. The gap between these two views of the child: the blank paper, or the active learner, is a constant thread in this book. Where I present examples of children learning where they appear to have got something wrong, or to have missed the point, I assume that some aspect of their thinking as active learners has subverted whatever they were asked to do.

Communication (inspired, to a large extent, of course, by love) concerns me most here. 'Babies', Wilkinson (1989) writes, 'are "conversationalists" before ever they can use language. They don't just make noises which other people interpret. They listen to other people, and respond to them, and make signals to which they expect responses.' Wilkinson has a vivid word-picture of a baby, sitting in her high chair, making 'a long impassioned speech in no recognisable language, banging a clenched fist, like a dictator at a rally after a coup d'etat'. As adults, we have always been, and still are, unwilling to conceptualise in ordinary life as learning that which we cannot see and understand entirely on our own terms. In other words, in the instance of Wilkinson's dictator-baby, we do not recognise readily how deep, how fast and how powerful the transformations, both intellectual and affective, are that are going on inside the child.

Children are active, not passive, in their need to tell us things, and to understand things that we tell them. Children are 'predisposed' (Wells 1986) to learn language, because they have patterns in their brains (as Chomsky saw it) that help them to make sentences. Evidence for this are those occasions when children make irregular verbs regular. They never hear an adult say 'I goed to the game', but children say it as they hypothesise what they should say to communicate something, because they are playing with a grammar (essentially, Chomsky says, subject + predicate) from the moment of their birth. See, for an introduction to this, Chomsky's (1972) essay 'Language and the mind'. Thus, the notion that children are, in terms of language, merely (I choose my adverb with care) a matter of imitating the talk of adults around them sells children and their learning powers absurdly short.

Throughout this book communication does not necessarily concern other people. Language is also about communicating with ourselves. Consider meditation. Consider the lists we make when we are in dispute with someone we love, or the notes we make to prepare ourselves for some important meeting, or the everlasting dialogues we have with ourselves about quite ordinary things. A reading of *Ulysses* by James Joyce will make this point clear. Here the hero, Leopold Bloom, reflects, late in the evening on his day, as most of us do, on what has occurred. This is a day when he's received a letter, had a public bath, listened to singing in a pub, had a row in another pub – all apart from adventures clear from the extract:

> Call to the hospital to see. Hope she's over. Long day I've had. Martha, the bath, funeral, house of keys, museum with those goddesses, Daedalus' song. Then that bawler in Barney Kiernan's. Got my own back there. Drunken ranters. What I said about God made him wince. Mistake to hit back? Or? No.

Early talk is (like *Ulysses*) a rediscovery of language. As the adult communicates with the child, and meets the child's hunger for communication, that adult acts as a teacher to an apprentice who is, from the beginning, aching to learn. There is a conviction that accompanies this: children should be treated as human beings who have related to, and understood, much of the world already. We usually pass on the nod the idea that children are experienced learners, but we frequently behave, like our ancestors, as though children were in fact blank slates; empty vessels. Two quotations from, respectively, a special needs teacher and an educational psychologist make this point: 'This child [a five-year-old] hasn't started yet.' 'We must stop him [a six-year-old] writing until he can form his letters properly.'

This book is, partly, an attack on the thinking behind remarks like these, which is concerned with control rather than respecting children and setting them free as active learners. On such thinking is built a deficit model that conceptualises children as lacking something. I prefer a model that sees children as human beings already advanced in their abilities and learning.

Structure of the book

The three-fold division in this book is, like most divisions in educational books, for convenience only; as Bearne (1995) points out, 'fragmentation of language impoverishes [and] narrows . . . Separating reading from writing can lead not only to frustration and concern about the nature and validity of assessments but, most importantly, to the danger of fragmenting children's language.' We have to bear in mind these dangers, and to cross-reference all three modes of language in all three sections. To fragment is also to control, to divide and rule, and the child set free in learning ranges over the convenient grid we as teachers impose on experience.

In Chapter 1 in Part I, I describe a three-year-old boy talking with his mother and myself. In Chapter 2 I present a case study of children talking in an infant classroom. Chapter 3 draws together children talking about various serious moral issues, including death. There is an interlude about children compiling and writing their own books. Part II is concerned with children writing. Chapter 4 is about writing generally. Chapters 5 and 6 comprise two studies, one of the writing corner, and the other of children writing letters. Chapter 7 is about children writing lists, and Chapter 8 is about spelling and related issues. Part III is about reading. Chapter 9 reflects on children facing print, and chapter 10 is about the politics of reading. Chapter 11 is about children and adults remembering how they learned to read. The books ends with a Postscript about the National Curriculum and an OFSTED (Office for Standards in Education) report on a school that figures throughout the book, Tacolneston in Norfolk.

Introducing Tacolneston First School

Throughout this book is threaded a document from an admirable first school in Norfolk. I had better explain why I admire this school so much, because that explanation will give away much about the stance of this book.

This small school (there are some thirty-odd children) is in the middle of a village about eight miles from Norwich. On my two-day visit there, in the summer of 1997, the walls were covered with material that stopped me at almost every point as I walked around: you simply wanted to look and read, and then examine further. Among many other things there were vivid paintings by the children, showing a confidence and assurance as well as a technical skill not to be found in all schools. The children had recently visited the nearby seaside town of Sheringham, and the paintings had an extra vigour because of that recent and powerful first-hand stimulus. Later, I saw this poem on a wall (Illustration 1):

I went to the sea and I found
a large pirate sword which made
me shiver.

I went to the sea and I found a scary shipwreck
which creaked
and groaned.

I went to the sea and I found a
dark cave
that constantly dripped
and the torchlight made the shapes
of sleeping bats
    bats hanging from
the ceiling
like leather rags.

I went to the sea and I found a
    fish bone
that moved.
It came right up to me.

This poem repays some examination. It is successful, it seems to me, for four reasons. The first is that it has a clear structure, presumably given to the writer by the teacher: the repetition of 'I went to the sea and I found . . . ' is the little cell that she has put a class of children in, aiming to stimulate the freeing of their imaginations. All art, as Leonardo said, needs a prison in order to be set free: mere writing about our feelings is usually formless and uninviting to the reader. Also it risks a kind of solipsism: writing that suggests to the reader that the writer and his or her obsessions are the only

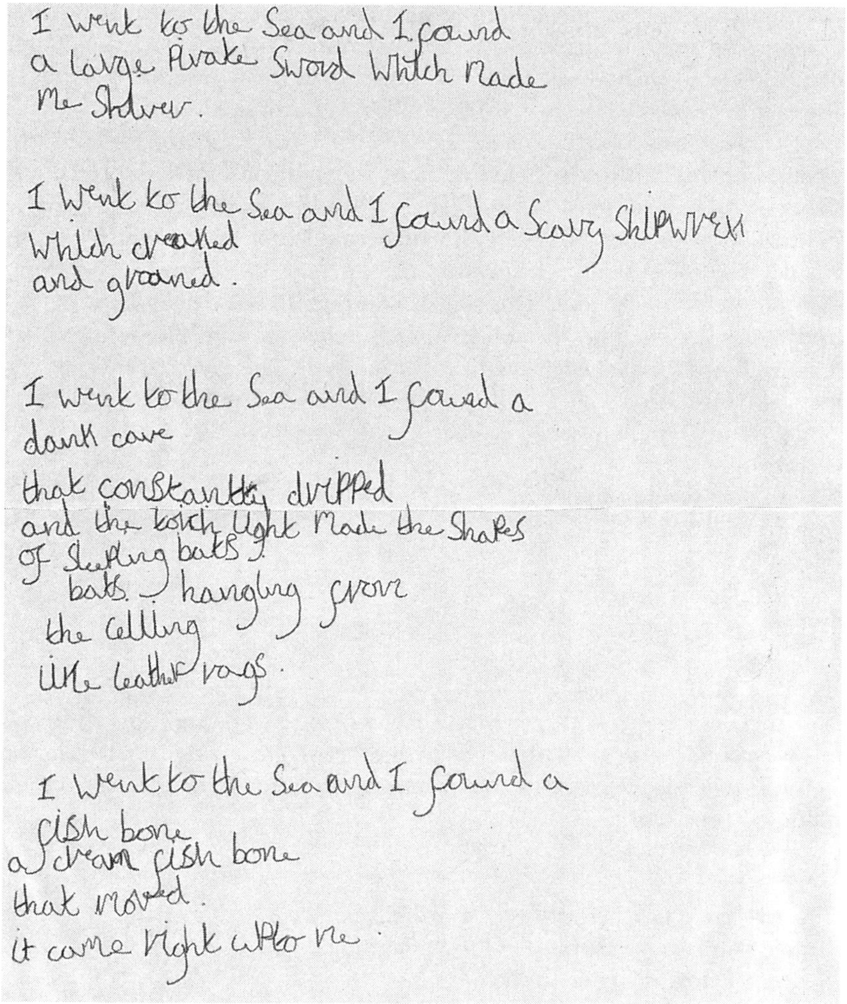

I went to the Sea and I found
a large Pirate Sword Which Made
Me Shiver.

I went to the Sea and I found a Scary Shipwreck
Which creaked
and groaned.

I went to the Sea and I found a
dark cave
that constantly dripped
and the torch light Made the Shapes
of sleeping bats
bats hanging from
the ceiling
like leather rags.

I went to the Sea and I found a
fish bone
a dream fish bone
that moved.
it came right up to me.

Illustration 1

things that count. Second, there is a ghostly presence behind this poem: e e cummings' 'maggie and milly and molly and may' (collected in, among other places, Heaney and Hughes 1982). Poems that are written by children with close recent and intense experience poetry are certain to be stronger than poems written (as so many are) outside the context of established poetry. Without such experience, how are children to either respond to the establishment's values, or react against them?

Third, the child has brought to the poem a lively experience of reading: this is obvious when we read 'the torchlight made the shapes/of sleeping bats/bats/hanging from/the ceiling/like leather rags'. In these lines is vivid evidence of having read metaphors; of having seen bats, or looked at pictures of them; of a partly-intuitive, partly-taught grasp of what cadence can do in a poem, associated with line endings. The experience this writer has brought to this poem is connected to the last reason for this poem's power: it was written in a school where words, visual images, first-hand experience and the responses of children to their environment were all constantly respected and celebrated; where, it must be said, such child-like responses were deemed infinitely more interesting than the managerial and administrative trivia demanded by the current bureaucratic structure.

Letters were important in this school. Authors like Anthony Browne had responded to letters from the children, and there were signed drawings from artists who had worked with them. After my visit, I received twenty letters. One said (Illustration 2):

> Dear Fred I
> love your powing I hope
> you come again
> you have macke my
> writing even better.
> Love from Jenna
> age 6

I note there especially 'you have macke my/writing *even* better': this child was already a confident writer. A letter from another six-year-old girl (Illustration 3) guilelessly ended 'I love you'. My favourite letter (for obvious reasons) went as follows (Illustration 4):

> Dear Fred
> I have got a bruther cold Fred But he is not a
> poet you have gathe me good idyes But my
> bruther Fred is a pane in the neck!!
> I liked the first one I did best
> I used to have a shark
> But
> now I am the Bait!
> love from William

I deal with this important matter of children corresponding in chapter 6.

One aspect of Tacolneston, less tangible than writing and art on walls, caused me to focus on the word 'respect'. There was no need here to bang wearisomely on (as generations and generations of adults in every culture have done) about children's respect for their teachers. This was partly because these were, largely, compliant children: they were the sort who 'did what they were told'. But they were not, ever, in my time with them, docile. They were free

Dear Fred I
Love your Powing I hope
You come a again
You have made my
writing even better.
Love From Jenna.
age 6

Illustration 2

with their opinions about many important things. The main reason for their (if I can define an educational ideal) *respectful openness* slowly became obvious to me: it was because the teachers *respected them*. These children understood, through the environment they were schooled in, that they mattered more to the teachers than the bits of paper the teachers were constantly having to fill in about them. This is not a universal state of affairs in our schools today.

There were photographs of the school's staff and children over the years, so that I looked at the teachers to see how much they had changed. To say that the teachers, classroom helpers and secretary that I studied myopically 'worked as a team' or 'pulled together' would expose the inadequacy of such clichés. The banter was of the kind that demonstrates the confidence they had, first, in their own abilities and, second, in each other. I felt sure that their confidence would protect them from whatever fortune. When I first visited the school, they told me that an OFSTED inspection loomed. You can find out

Dear Fred
I like you weh you
can it woe god
weh you can you did
poelms and I like
myn az wel
I LOVe you
Love From Annabele

Illustration 3

Dear Fred
I have got a bruther cold Fred But He is not a
poet you have gathe me good dyes But my
bruther Fred is a Pane in the hek!!
I liked the first one I did best
I used to have a shark est
But now I am the bait!
love from william

Illustration 4

at the end of this book how a language- and art-oriented school fared in that inspection; how a school that had many of the marks of the Plowdenesque 1960s, without the sentimentality of that decade, would fare when faced with the banal managerialism of the late 1990s.

Tacolneston School's English policy is threaded throughout this book.

16

Part I

CHILDREN AND TALK

1

EARLY TALK

In this chapter, I use a case study of Alastair, a three-year-old boy, to open issues of control and freedom in talk at home. First, I place the notion of early talk in the context of humankind's linguistic origins, as seen in myth, pre-history and theory. I then widen the context to include modern writers who have listened closely to children talking.

The story of the Tower of Babel (Genesis 11: 1–9) teaches us, among other things, that humankind aims to gain power over the environment through language, and that, by the same token, we are aware that there is a price to pay for such aspirations. And a child asks, on being requested to say what troubles her most, 'why do people talk different?'

'Speech is the representation of the experiences of the mind', Aristotle told us ('On Interpretation'). In other words, language has a kind of one-to-one relationship with thought. Something like this view of the matter lasted among experts until the seventeenth century, but we now know that it is an over-simplification. To watch humans using language is to throw up all kinds of complex notions about what is going on, not least the considerations that language itself has some considerable impact on thought. Also, it is not always to do with thought at all ('Damn!' 'How are you?') and where it is, language is a means for thought itself: are we able to conceptualise what we have no words for? Humankind's rationality developed alongside the development of the capacity for speaking, for language.

That is why clarity and openness in public language are so important. Sloppy, dishonest sentences in finished speeches, books and articles are sometimes the results of sloppy thought, and lead to, in turn, sloppier thought still, and at other times are the result of very precise thought aimed at deception. I once said to an Italian in a hotel swimming pool in his own country how beautiful his language is, and he replied that yes, it was, and it was a good language to lie in. To some extent this is true of all language: politicians and advertisers use the attractiveness of language: its rhythm, its

19

alliteration, its rhyme, its assonance, its repetition, to persuade us, and often the elegance of language is being used to stop us looking at other aspects of the subject that might disturb us.

While loose language in public is evidence of a will to prevaricate, in thinking, and in first drafts, it is the result of something quite different, something that is essentially creative: thoughts that float from one association to another make connections between things previously seen as disparate. This connection is the essence of two of the most potent uses of language: humour (the surprise in the punchline) and poetry (the surprise in the metaphor).

For some thinkers, notably behaviourist psychologists, thought is subvocal speech: merely an activity that prepares for a greater one, a more significant one. This is a disturbing notion, because if the person sitting thinking in a chair is pre-speech, or sub-speech, thought is devalued. When we try to reason through a problem – where to put access to an extension in the loft, for example, or how to develop a new curriculum in a school maximising the richness not only of the children's experiences, but also the teachers', our solving of that problem is seen in these terms as merely preparation for observable behaviour. That is bad enough.

But make the problem something more important, such as a decision about a relationship, or religious meditation, and we can see that the notion of thought as subvocal will not do. At the furthest extreme, it makes philosophy and theology irrelevant – and education, also, at least as it is distinguished from training. Education opens out infinite possibilities: training narrows all possibilities down to one. Education is concerned with a human being's autonomy: training is concerned with how the relatively powerful in society can use the relatively weak. Education deals with a countryside of mountains, hills, valleys, plains, rivers, lakes, beaches: training deals with a railtrack leading inexorably to a fixed point. Schools are necessarily concerned with both, because they must train children to be safe, but when we talk about language, we can be concerned only with education, with the opening out of possibilities.

This chapter is made up of a case study of three-year-old Alastair's talk. Drawing on Tizard and Hughes (1984) and Wells (1986), who have many eloquent examples of children talking at home, exploring intellectually questions that are vital to them, I show here how the child I recorded was intent on discovery; in dread of misunderstanding things. I have noted elsewhere, with my wife, how complex children's early sentences often are in contrast to what they are asked to read (Sedgwick and Sedgwick 1996) and also how serious some children's early talk is. For example: a three year old, my son, was watching his pram being put away in the loft: 'Are you keeping that for when I'm a baby again?' Another example: the same child, now a five year old: 'How do we know the world began with a big bang when there weren't any scientists around, not even dinosaur scientists?' And another three year old: 'What's in your hand, Mummy? – Nothing. What's in my hand? –

Nothing. – . . . Is the nothing that's in my hand the same as the nothing that's in yours? . . . Nah, it's a different nothing.' The same three year old asked his father about the elderly people living in sheltered accommodation opposite their house. He was told 'When you are old, and have no one to look after you, you might go and live in those homes.' Later the little boy saw the Wheelie bins being collected from across the street. The street is a boundary between local authorities, and the Wheelie bins on the opposite side are green, while those where the boy's family lives are black. He said to his father, watching the refuse collection: 'If no one loves you, you have green bins. If they do, you have black ones.'

Pat Czerniewska (1992) offers examples of children talking and suggests that such talk can teach us, but this is a relatively recent notion. There is a contrast between our conventional attitude to such utterances with our attitude to spelling. The first we see as cute, or ignore them; the second we become obsessive about. If we take this kind of behaviour to extremes, we will teach children something that we do not want them to learn: that what they say to us in day-to-day conversations over the dinner table, or walking in the park, is less important than the correspondence of their spelling to current conventions. Our first job as teachers of language is to pay attention; to be, as Czerniewska suggests, a learner. Wells (1986) says of a child, Rosie, who was deemed a failure at school, 'When provided with the support of a listener who was interested in what *she* had to say, Rosie was no longer incompetent.'

There are, according to Wells, four principles to consider about how adults can help children with their language. The first is to treat what the child has to say as worthy of careful attention. This notion of attention is very powerful, I think. Simone Well (Panichas 1977) writes 'Never in any case whatever is a genuine effort of attention wasted . . . Without our knowing it or feeling it, this apparently barren effort [of attention on some impenetrable subject] has brought more light into the soul'; elsewhere she shows us that love is simply the giving of our complete attention to someone who needs it. And, as Wells (1986) says, the children acquiring fluency and power over language need that attention, that unsentimental love, as much as anyone. It is interesting to note this is a reversal of the old school principle, that it is the pupils who should be paying attention to the teacher. Like the notion of respect, attention has to go in two directions simultaneously if it is to have the kind of quality than makes it work.

Wells' second principle is also concerned with attention: to do one's best to understand what the child means. This requires considerable effort at times, but it is worth it, because of the third principle: to take the child's meaning as the basis for what to say next. This is simply offering the child the control of the agenda, and, therefore, offering him or her the opportunity to learn what is necessary now. The fourth principle is that in selecting and encoding one's message, take account of the child's ability to understand – that is, to construct an appropriate interpretation.

Alastair[1]

Alastair was three years old when I first recorded a conversation with him. I reproduce parts of it here, with comments, partly based on Wells' four principles.

Fred: What's your name?

Right at the beginning, we note afterwards, something problematical happens. And while in teaching/learning settings, it is usually assumed that the problem is posed by the child, here it is the teacher, me, asking a silly question. Alastair knows I know his name. So why am I asking him? Let this question stand here for all the unreal questions teachers ask children. By unreal, I mean questions that are really something else: 'What do you think you're doing?' 'Would you do that at home?' 'How many times do I have to tell you . . .'. An example of an inappropriate question is in this conversation:

Teacher [to class with OFSTED inspector present]:   Today we are going to learn about . . . [explains at length subject of lesson]
Later, OFSTED inspector [to six year old]:   And what are you learning about?
Child [reproachfully, to inspector]:   Someone wasn't listening!

Alastair did not respond 'But you know my name!' because he is too well mannered, too socialised into the ways of the adult world, one of which tells him that he treats silly questions seriously. The tape continues:

Alastair: That's a funny thing [recording machine]. That's a funny thing.
F: What do you think it is?
A: I think it is . . . . [long pause] Daddy's at school . . . He's gonna do some work.
F: What sort of work? [long pause] Do you like it when Daddy goes to school to do some work?
A: Yeh.
F: Do you like it when he comes home? What do you say when he comes home?
Cindy   (Alastair's mother):   What do you say to Daddy?
A: I love you!
C: Ah that's nice!
F: And what does he say to you? Does he give you a hug? [s]
C: You say 'Daddy's home'.
A: I say 'Daddy's home'.

---

1 In all transcriptions of tapes, * = inaudible and s= silence.

In this part of the transcript, Alastair must be confused, and with very good reason. He has never had a conversation like this, with two adults, one not his father, bringing subjects – his name, his feelings about Daddy going to work, conversations with his Daddy – out of the blue into the room. And the one who is not his father has a little black box making a hissing noise. Suddenly, using a toy, that from now on he rumbles across the little table, where we are talking, he breaks free of this weird stuff:

A: That's a digger and that's another digger that's another digger that's another digger.
C: How does the one on the back work?
A: Yeh.
C: How does the one on the back work? Does it *
A: Yeh.
C: *** What kind of noise does it make?
[long silence]
A: Yeah! [he plays as Cindy and I talk. Then]
F: . . . What do you do in the park?
A: I go down the slide.
F: Do you go fast down the slide?
A: No.
F: What do you do?
A: I [?]draw a big one.
F: On the big slide.

This subject meanders out. I don't think I have acknowledged sufficiently here Wells' second principle, to try to understand; as a direct result, of course, I cannot take Alastair's meaning as a basis for what to say next.

A: My finger's stuck [it might've been . . . it wasn't] It's raining! [it wasn't]
F: What are those men doing?
A: Hammering.
C: Can you see a crane?
A: I see a crane [shout].
F: What did it do?
A: It got some water.
F: What did it do with the water? What did it do with the water?
A: Er.
[long pause]
F: It doesn't matter.
A: No.
F: Would you like to have a go with the sand and water?
A: No.

Cindy and Alastair together, later the same day

C: You gonna make a little man for me?
A: Yeh.
C: What kind of a man is he? What's he made out of? [s] What's he made out of? [s] What's that? Mm? Does this man have a – does he have a nose?

It is striking here how demanding Cindy is in her questioning. She is also a teacher, and perhaps that is part of the reason.

A: Yeh.
C: Where's his nose? Show me his nose.
A: Right there.
C: Right there. What's that you just put on? Mm? What's that there?
A: ** another little man.
C: OK good, you'll make a new one . . . Does that man have a name? What's his name?
A: Dawn.
C [surprised]: His name is Dawn.

This is my wife's name. Alastair is making a connection between three things: his conversation earlier, when I was present, times we have visited the family, and this conversation. Are we paying attention? Because if we are, we will think again about assumptions that children at this age lack so much. Later on, Alastair will bring my son Daniel into the conversation. This shows that conversations contain more things than we are aware of; that a behaviouristic description of a conversation will necessarily leave out much of interest. If we think for a time about our own conversations, and the way they move from one subject to an unrelated one, we can see something similar happening.

C: And does he have, does he have . . . glasses? [Cindy is guessing that Dawn is, in fact, me]
A: Yeh.
C: Where are his glasses? There. Where's he gonna go today? Where's this playdough man gonna go today?
A: To school.
C: He's gonna go to school? What's he do when he gets to school?
A: He's gonna get that wheelbarrow.
C: Oh. What does he do with that?
A: He's gonna put some mud in it.
C: He's gonna put some mud in the wheelbarrow? Does he take it somewhere?
A: Yeh.

C: Where does he take it?
[s]
C: So. Does the man push the wheelbarrow somewhere?
A: Yeh.
C [rapid]: Where does he push it? Mm? Does Daddy have a wheelbarrow?
A: Yeh?
C: Where does Daddy push his wheelbarrow? Where does Daddy push his
    wheelbarrow? [s]
C: Did you help Daddy with the wheelbarrow one day?

Here are more questions, rapidly fired at Alastair.

A: Yeh.
C: What did you do with it?
A: Daddy put some *
C: Daddy put * in it? Where did you put it?
A: I put it away.
C: You put it away for him? And then what did you do?
A: Get some more.
C: Get some more. What was Daddy doing?
A: He was weeding.
C: Oh!
A: In the garden.
C: You took all the weeds out of the garden. Where do you put them? Mm?
A: On the wheelbarrow
C: Do you like to help Daddy?
A: Yes.
C: What's this?
A: Man.
C: There's a man. Where's your man? Is that your man?
A: Yes.
C: What's he doing today? What's your man doing today? Whoops I must *
    there. [s] Is that his head whoops! Put it back on. Put his head on.
A: Yes.
C: Put his head on. Oh, what did you do to his head? What did you do to
    that head?
A: ?gonna make a new head.
C: OK. Does this one have a name? What's his name? What's his name?
***
C: You took his head off. Oh you put it back on again. What's that man
    going to do today? What's he going to do? Is he going to go somewhere?
    What's that man going to do, go somewhere? [s] Is he gonna go
    somewhere? Oh. He's a flat man now isn't he?
A: Yeh.

25

C: Which part of him is that?
A: He's a fat man!
C: He's a fat man! Where are his legs?
A: There.
C: Does he walk somewhere?
A: Yeh.
C: Where does he walk to?
A: To Dan.
C: To Dan? What does he do when he gets to Dan's house? What does he do when he gets to Dan's house?
A: Actually, he's going [long pause] he's going he's going – Oh swish swish – he's going to the park.
C: What's he going to do when he gets to the park? What's he going to when he gets to the park?

A little more about these questions. They are unrelenting, they are often repeated, and when one is answered, it leads inevitably to another question: 'he's going to the park . . . What's he going to when he gets to the park? What's he going to when he gets to the park?'

A: Fish.
C: What's he going to when he gets to the park? Is he going to play on something?
A: Yeh.
C: What is going to play on? [s] Or is he going to go for a walk first? . . . Can you make, you make another ball? You want me to make another ball? OK. What are you going to with this ball? What are you going to with this ball? What's this? [s] What shall we make?
[s] [working?]
A: I'm taking him to the park.
C: Oh OK. What are you going to do with him when you get to the park? Does he have to hold your hand when you go to the park?
A: He does.
C: What do you do when you go to the park?
A: I hold your hand.
C: Yes you do, that's right, you hold my hand. And then once we get in the gates you're allowed to run around, aren't you?
A: Yes.

In the first conversation, I try to let Alastair dictate the agenda. For example, when he points to the recorder and says, 'That's a funny thing, that's a funny thing' I ask him 'What do you think it is?' I go along with his interests. In school I would have brushed this aside and got on with what I considered the real business of the meeting. And yet, as Wells says, learning happens best when we go along with what the child says. Later, Cindy readily allows Alastair to change the subject from love of his Daddy to the digger he wants to play with.

There are, in fact, two schemes in any conversation of this type. There is the adult's, which is often concerned with what that adult sees as the child's potential learning, and is here concerned, as well, with understanding the child's learning and trying to record some of it; and there is the child's scheme. In these transcripts Alastair often dictates the conversation, changing items when something serious comes up: the digger for example, and the invention about his finger being stuck. Sometimes he says things that aren't true, but they widen the perspectives of the conversation to his benefit. He uses fillers ('yeh') and silence to bring the conversation to his concerns. On the other hand, Cindy interrogates Alastair. Walkerdine and Lucey (1989) interpret this in terms of the pressure on middle-class mothers to be pedagogues. When one collects the questions together, we can see considerable teacherly pressure being applied to Alastair:

> What kind of a man is he? What's he made out of? What's he made out of? What's that? Mm? Does this man have a – does he have a nose? Where's his nose? Show me his nose. Does that man have a name? What's his name? Where are his glasses? Where's he gonna go today? Where's this playdough man gonna go today?

But much of this pressure came from me: no researcher is ever researching purely his or her setting. Researchers are always researching the setting as affected by themselves. And I can stand here as a symbol for society's demands on mothers at home.

A year later I spoke to Alastair again. When I arrived, Duncan, Alastair's father, told me that 'at the moment, Alastair is interested in the wrong trousers'. Later, the boy walked into the room with large marching strides, intoning as he went along: 'I am the wrong trousers.' His language had acquired great fluency; he listened to poems with attention, and constantly asked for them to be said again. All the learning evident in this conversation, which I do not reproduce here, was generated by himself and his parents at home, as well as other relatives and friends. School had, as yet, had nothing to do with it. The question I asked myself as I left was, what would school do with his learning? With the wrong trousers? It would be a while before I knew the answer – Alastair was still only four – but I went to a school to see how children talked there, and how I as a teacher talked with them, and listened to them.

2

TALK IN THE INFANT SCHOOL

In this chapter, I use a case study of infants talking in a small junior mixed infant school to explore further issues of freedom and control. Before that, I discuss teachers' reactions to research that suggests that schools tend to deaden children's talk rather than enliven it.

The speaking and listening part of the English policy at Tacolneston school says that

The Literate Child (who leaves our school at 8 years of age) should be able to

- Listen with discernment, and enter into conversation with empathy;
- Express their views and opinions;
- Ask meaningful questions, and see other people's points of view;
- Use talk to think, plan, negotiate and reflect.

I listen to talk in schools against the background of a remark of Flanders that I came across while studying with the Open University in 1974. The rule of two-thirds tells us that two-thirds of every lesson is taken up with talk; that two-thirds of that talk is teacher talk; and that, therefore, in a three-quarter-hour session involving thirty pupils, each will talk for twenty seconds. As Cashdan *et al.* (1972) say 'this cannot be thought long enough for exploratory thought'. My own listening would suggest that something very like two-thirds of teacher talk is actually administrative, managerial or disciplinary in character, rather than educational; and that much of the child-talk is merely in response to such talk.

What follows (it originally appeared in an earlier draft in *Montessori Education*) is intended as a warning about what we as teachers devalue in homes. It has a special resonance in the light of the paucity of educational child-talk in schools. The teachers' uncritically accepted assumption that children don't have good language experiences at home (unlike in some golden era when children sat with their parents discussing Wittgenstein and the music of the second Vienna school) might, with more justification, be reversed. If parents knew about the state of affairs in schools with regard to the amount and quality of children's talk, they might be alarmed.

Nil on entry

Whether you're a teacher, a nursery nurse or a student, or some other worker in the Montessori vineyard, I wonder what you think of, or feel about, these three statements:

- 'the [nursery] school's curriculum is considerably narrower than the home's'
- 'passages of intellectual search' by children are 'entirely absent at the [nursery] school'
- children 'have a much greater familiarity with language than one would expect from listening to [their] conversations [with teachers] in nursery schools'

To attempt to sum up these huge claims, I would say: adult–child conversations in homes are educationally richer than they are in nursery schools. In fact, the argument that contains these words is even more startling in its entirety, because it says that conversations in working-class homes (defined in various ways) are educationally richer than conversations in schools. Before you go any further, perhaps you could note mentally or, even better, on paper your reactions.

* * *

Barbara Tizard and Martin Hughes (1984) said these things in their book. They showed that parents teach more than teachers believe they do. As Hughes (1989) puts it in a later article 'the homes of working-class children, far from being arid deserts as is often supposed, were in fact a rich source of learning opportunities . . . most young children start school with considerable intellectual capacities'. So, there is a gap between school and home – but not in the way it's usually conceived. Forget the deficit, the notion that children fail in school because of lack of motivation, inadequate home socialisation and poverty of language. That, as Valencia (1997) says, is a 'pseudo-science' founded on race and class bias. By contrast, the school–home gap appears as follows.

There is more adult talk per child at home, and less at school. This is in part for an obvious reason: there are always far fewer children playing with mother or (less often) father round the kitchen table, modelling with playdough or making things with Duplo or whatever it might be, than there are round the water or sandtrays in the classroom. Thus children at home have more of an adult's time than they do at school. But, more importantly, the quality of the talk at home is better. It is livelier and more vigorous, more relevant to the child's current needs. I've noted this in examples from my work with children. At his home, I let my godson James follow his own important agenda. At school, by contrast, because of my (or the National Curriculum's) requirement, I cut children off just as they are approaching something important to them. But, for that very reason, the fact that they are approaching something important, learning is likely to be at its most effective.

Despite this research (and our own less formal experiences), most of us teachers believe that working-class homes are barren as bomb sites in all areas that matter, and especially in language. One teacher said to Hughes (1989) that some children come to school with 'nil on entry'. The blood runs cold at such dismissive, destructive arrogance. Teachers assume that children, may, in general, in other parts of the town, or city, or county, or country or world have good experiences of language at home. But not 'round here'. And 'not in this catchment area'.

Martin Hughes has more evidence that such perception of language in working-class homes is wrong. He and his colleagues found that parents saw their children as chatterboxes ('he never stops' and 'she rabbits on and on') while teachers were saying things like 'they say very little . . . they haven't begun to talk very fluently'. How can both assessments be true? We must assume that something happens in schools that turns talkers into non-talkers. To quote the principle at the heart of the Reggio-Emilia approach to children in their early years, 'children have at their disposal a hundred languages, of which the school steals ninety-nine' (Drummond 1998).

I notice this when I talk to children about a passion of theirs – fishing, or horse-riding. They talk freely, readily and, most importantly, accurately, using technical words. Often, the same children in school are silent. One of the languages – the one that has 'trout', 'line', 'reel', 'bridle', 'gallop', 'bit' in its lexicon – has been stolen from them. To be what Drummond (following Japanese usage) calls a 'child-like child' with a passion for a non-school subject has been disallowed. The child becomes a user of one institutional language, a mere imitator of elders and betters and a victim of a massive disrespect.

Tape recordings made in homes by Tizard and Hughes showed that 'a large amount of talk was taking place in children's homes, covering a wide range of topics'. There were examples of children 'explaining' and examples of children 'listening'. There was evidence that children were familiar at home with general knowledge (again, flying in the face of many teachers' assumptions) such as the names of colours and numbers. And the children also seemed familiar with nursery rhymes and stories.

Despite there being less adult talk at school, it was more adult-dominated, being, all too often, managerial, disciplinary and administrative. Questions asked – 'Will you make sure you've done that before we do this? . . . Would you do that at home? . . . Please could you open that window?' construct a contrasting context from the one the children are used to at home. This is one of the reasons for the difference between the perceptions of parents on the one hand and teachers on the other. And the new context in which children find themselves is what turned some of them into non-talkers. Much teacher talk, arguably, has nothing to do with teaching. You can test this with a tape recorder in your classroom: take a sample of ten minutes of your talk, transcribe it. Then assess it with the following questions in mind:

- Was this talk educational?
- Was it administrative? (about registers, closing windows or doors, etc.)
- Was it disciplinary?
- Were the questions real ones (that is, questions you didn't already know the answer to) or were they checks on what the children knew?

This last question has to be seen in relation to the fact that most questions at home (Would you like some more chips? Are you coming with me to the shops or staying at home with Daddy? Do you like your new puppy?) are very different from most of the questions at school. This, incidentally, explains what sounds like rudeness in a school starter, when it is merely responding to questions as if they were home questions, that is, real ones: Would you like to sit on the carpet? No. This is all part of the changed context in which children see, hear and learn language at school.

The same problems are there in writing in schools, too. I was in a school where children were turned, potentially at least, into non-writers by the simple disrespectful trick of not letting them write any word until they could spell it properly. The following story (Illustration 5), composed independently on a computer by a six year old in a very different school, would not have been allowed in that school – let's call it Stalin County Primary – because the boy would have had to check each spelling before he'd written a word.

What has George done here that is more important than immaculate spelling and grammar? First, he has shown some understanding of narrative. Second, he has used that narrative to think about issues that matter to him: family relations, jeering, girls, poverty, being lost. The fact that he has not written down all his thoughts about these things is irrelevant. Third, he has used the computer to express his love for his grandparents. All this would have been closed to George at Stalin County Primary, where he would have been in a Gulag with a motto: if you can't spell it, don't write it. Once again, several languages would have been stolen from a child: his narrative, his

> Thursday 30 th October
> One time ther was a caveman. He did not have a wife.
> But he had a boy. The boys name was Tom.The
> caveman did not have a name. One day the caveman
> was poor. Tom said ha ha ha. Shut up said the
> c ave man. No said Tom. Yes you will said the
> caveman.So tom stopd.A girl was there. Tom kissed
> the girl.The girl kissed tom. What is your name. I am
> toni. I am lost. we will help you if you give us sume
> money. Toni had sume money in her pocket.. Toni
> gave the caveman 10 p. The caveman toock toni to her
> mum.. The caveman bought some food. THE END. Dear
> grandma and Grandad I hope you ar ok. My next
> door neighbour came over to play at my house. You
> to ar my best frens. xxxx all thos x is ar kiss is.
> Lots of love George J.R.

Illustration 5

affectionate words for his grandparents, his tentative exploration of emotional difficulties.

Teachers' reactions

What do teachers say when faced with this research? What did you say above? Typically, we all reject it. I gave most infant teachers that I met during a term three comments from Tizard and Hughes (1984) I have quoted on p. 29.

One typical response says

> The second statement (unfortunately) is totally untrue of this catchment area, where the majority of children's knowledge appears to come from the school – even the basics of speech, colours, numbers etc . . . and the third . . . not at all . . . problem solving in drama, reading of poetry, listening comprehensions, descriptive books and passages, reading of 'great' literature, discussion and questioning.

Another says in answer to the first comment

Children's language in communication, especially understanding of language, seems to be getting poorer. Listening skills and understanding of vocabulary is poor.

and to the second

No! Children entering school have very few book skills – left to right etc. Not much knowledge of nursery rhymes, traditional stories.

In answer to the third comment this respondent said simply, 'No, lots of information, picture books'. Other parents commented that none of the children knew what a saucer was. This is a matter of context again. How many children (or their parents, for that matter) use saucers day by day? We don't in our house.

What are the reasons for teachers disagreeing so vehemently with the researchers' findings? We are mostly middle-class people and have an understandable, if largely unacknowledged, bias in favour of our own background; we assume that to grow up in bought (or, more likely, mortgaged) housing, with parents in white-collar occupations, gives us advantages in our learning. In fact, the real advantages, as working-class students at university know, is more realistically seen in terms of social acceptance.

These assumptions lead to arrogance: the notion that children have rich language experiences at home is 'totally untrue of this catchment area, where the majority of children's knowledge appears to come from the school'.

There is a failure to understand what context implies. I have already noted how different the place of questions is in the two significant places in a child's life. Also, children are suddenly faced with a context where 'skills' are dominant. Does a fluent reader think of his or her ability to read a novel or the newspaper in terms of skills? Why should a child? Or a child's teacher/parents?

There was a joke going around staffrooms a few years ago, in the early days of the AIDS scare. One child to another: Last night we found a condom on the patio. Other child: What's a patio? This pretends to be a story about childish ignorance about nice things (patios) and gratuitous knowledge about nasty ones (condoms). Children may be language deprived around here, but they know about sex! But I read it as a story about a teacher's perceived moral superiority. We see here a clash between a culture – let's call it a patio-culture that, for various reasons I'd rather not write about just now, and a condom-culture, which may be not nice to the patio-people, but which is grounded in the daily realities of life, and in the fact that, however we might try to protect children from those realities, they are conscious of horrors and glories the world holds in store for them. In any case, I'd rather my child-like child knew about condoms than patios.

It is striking that many of the Tizard and Hughes parents actually use the word 'teach' when discussing their conversations with their children, while teachers, in contrast, typically, talk about 'providing a learning environment'. One corollary to this is that parents often say to nursery teachers (as one has just said to my wife) 'of course, we know you don't teach them anything. . . . like reading and writing and arithmetic'. Parents seem to accept implicitly that more teaching happens at home than at school, and in a wider curriculum. Of course, this begs the question of what we mean by teaching. A generation of teachers grew up professionally in the 1960s and 1970s believing that they were not, in one sense of the word, teachers at all, but providers of environmental factors that would make learning more likely, or enablers of learning. They 'bathed children in language'. This disguised the fact that teaching is unavoidable. First, the provision of environmental factors was an act of teaching. Second, there was a great deal more teacher talk, explicit teaching going on than we owned up to. When we try as teachers to talk less, to enable the children to talk more, we are still teachers. In a decent society everyone would want to be a teacher, while the rest would have to be satisfied with minor jobs, like prime minister and adviser and inspector.

Go back, briefly, to Alastair. Did he possess nil on entry? Could such a phrase ever be sufficiently respectful of him and his contemporaries?

Six year olds talking

What follows is a transcript of some six year olds in a primary school, Tattingstone County Primary in Suffolk. In many ways, this school resembles Tacolneston: a vivid, exciting environment, with easy-going respectful relationships between the teachers and the children. Given that similarity, the schools are different from each other, because they are passionate schools, and like all such schools, they are their own schools, and not like other ones. Both, though, are marvellous. I have written about Tattingstone before (Sedgwick 1993:44 ff), and any one interested in the context of what follows might find my earlier account helpful. The school resembles a cross between a secular community of learners and an artist's studio.

The children on this tape are Justin, Daniel, Helena, Thomas and Jesse.

I bring a dark African carving out (Illustration 6). It represents a woman and children, the children clambering all around the woman. The school children talk together about it. Hubbub: 'Got your – I know – '. Then

FS: Hang on a minute. Hang on a minute. What's your name?

Oh no! The same question that I asked Alastair, but this time genuine, because I don't know this boy's name. But why this obsession with names? You write your name nervously first thing at the top of an examination paper;

34

Illustration 6

indeed, it is a common myth that you'll get one mark for it. No wonder these children behaved as though they were being tested: they had already faced the test battery that the system fires at them. And to name names is to establish control. The Cherokee Indians, beginning here like a teacher, knew that:

> Listen!
> Now I have come to step over your soul
> (I know your clan)

35

(I know your name)

. . .

I bury your soul under earth.
                    (Causley 1974)

And I can, like any efficient teacher, snap a name and silence things.

Daniel: Daniel {rising intonation, as if being arrested}
FS: What are you gonna say Daniel?
Daniel: I think, the erm, it's from where –
Justin: Let's find it –

Justin always wants to get things right.

            – you know, where the pyramids are
FS: Where's that?

(another example of an unreal question)

Daniel: Can't remember now
FS: Where's that?

(repetition as control)

Jesse: Egypt.
FS: What do you think? You tell me about that.
Helena: Um. It looks like, um, a dead person.
FS: How d'you mean?
Thomas: A Mummy.
FS: So you're thinking about the pyramids as well
            [hubbub] {Egypt . . . What about you? . . .}
FS: Hang on a minute, one at a time
Daniel: Well, Egypt statue, I think it's an Egypt statue –
FS: Egypt statue. Go on.
Daniel: from when er somebody died they put their, some, person that they
            made it, they made a wood thing and they said it was a person.
FS: Right. Thank you Daniel. Justin. You tell me what you were going
            to say –

This exchange, I remind myself on the twentieth plus reading, is between an
experienced teacher/researcher and young children. And yet still I say 'Right.
Thank you Daniel', closing down the opportunity for Daniel to explore
further a notion that looks to me now to be far more interesting than I
evidently thought it then.

Justin:	Well, we don't know who the person is do we. Y'see . . . is in Egypt and we don't know who all these people are sitting around her – ***
FS:	Can I ask Helena what do you think about this?
Helena:	If they found a person that's dead, and they might have made, laid it down and then made a statue of it
FS:	What do you think?
Helena:	That might be a famous person, so they put it in wood . . . and gave one to all the people in Egypt.

What a fantastic notion this is! And yet this experienced teacher/researcher dismisses it thus:

FS:	You go, you all go along with the Egyptian idea. [Yeh they say]. Tell me this, tell me this [almost whispering]. Can I show you something? Can you look at the lady's face
?	yes its * its *
FS:	Look what she's doing. I'm going to pass it round can you hold it. Look at the children, feel them as well . . . What's that lady –
Helena:	It's heavy –
FS:	What's going through her head? Jesse. What's she thinking about?
Jesse:	Thinking about all her children.
FS:	Yeh, I reckon she might – what's she thinking about those children?
Helena:	They might die?
FS:	She's thinking they might die. Do you think mummies think that about their children?
Helena:	Yeah. Cos if they haven't got anything to eat –
FS:	Mmmm-
Helena:	And anything to drink they might die.
FS:	Mmmm. What do you think she's thinking about Daniel?
Daniel:	Same as Helen.
FS:	What are those children up to?
	[inaudible hubbub]
Helena:	Climbing up her
Daniel	[in a rush]: The children didn't like the other mummies and they went to this mummy and they climbed all over her because they liked her.
FS:	Can I just get that right. Did you say, er, 'they went to this mummy and they climbed all over her because they liked her'?
Daniel:	Mm.
FS:	Right!

This is a worry. Daniel has expressed an idea that, for reasons I can't now explore, I am interested in, and I reinforce it so positively, demonstrating the behaviourist teaching techniques we are all imbued with, that all Daniel can say is, 'Mm'. My enthusiastic repeat has dumbfounded him. See it from his point of view: what's behind this sudden rush from Sir? Have I given something away about my life? I think I'll shut up now, to be on the safe side.

FS:	How does it feel for this lady – you don't have to answer straight-away – How does it feel for this lady to have all those children climbing all over her?
Helena:	Heavy.
FS:	Anything else?
Thomas:	Terrible * trembling.
FS:	Trembling?
Thomas:	* all around her.
FS:	What all around her?
Justin:	Scattering all around her cos they're all over her.
FS:	'Scattering all around her'. Lovely phrase [to Duncan, the headteacher, in the room]. 'Scattering all around her'.
Daniel:	They're everywhere.
Justin:	It's like a ladder.
FS:	It's like a ladder! She's a ladder?
Justin:	He's carrying something in a basket.
	[hubbub]
FS:	Justin's on to something here, look, Justin's on to something here. Can you say that again Justin so everyone can hear?
Justin:	He's carrying something.
	[discussion here about what's in the basket: cabbage, a rock that's been chopped off, carrots, lettuce]
FS:	Tell you what. Tell you what [gaining control, leading to required silence]. I'm going to ask you something and I don't want you to answer until I've snapped my fingers cos that'll make you think for a minute. Don't answer straightaway. Tell me some of the ways the person who made this did his or her work.
Justin:	Oh goodness me! No!
FS:	Have a feel with your fingers. Tell me some of the ways this person did his or her work.
	[pause]
	OK? [snap of fingers]
FS:	Jesse.
Jesse:	He put patterns on, like stripes and all these.
FS:	How did he do that?
Jesse:	By um. By getting a screwdriver and going THAT way and THAT way.
FS:	What do you say Helena?

38

Helena:	Well it feels a bit rough so that I think first that he or her she did it rough and then he or she did it really carefully.
FS:	What tools do you think SHE used then?
Helena:	Screwdrivers.
FS:	I've never seen – Have you ever used a screwdriver in your art lessons?

[Hubbub. No! said by several. Never! Never used tools.]

FS:	What tools would you have used to make something like this?
Jesse:	Chipped it.
Daniel:	I'd get a chipper and I'd get the edge of it and chip the rest of it out.
FS:	Some pieces aren't chipped, how do you think this part was made [the face, all smooth].
Daniel:	Well they got a sandpaper, and they sanded it. And they all, and that all came up like that.

At this point I announced I was leaving the room, and yet I'd like to know what they say. They knew about the Dictaphone. (You see this little box, I don't want you to touch it – You're taping our voices!) I told them that when I came back I ask them what they'd been talking about, but I didn't do this, in fact. I suggested some questions they might like to consider, about what she was thinking, about how it was made, and about the expressions on the children's faces.

Justin:	Everyone look at this [carving] all right and no talking about this [Dictaphone, presumably]. I'll start off, right cos –
?	All right, all right, let's get this done cos these people here [hubbub]
Daniel:	I'm the youngest!
	[hubbub] [he's six, he's seven]
Helena:	Shhhh!
?	I'll go, Jesse.
	[huge sigh from someone – frustration, I think]
Justin:	Can we please just get on with this?
Daniel:	* up to her.
Justin:	All right, Daniel; all right.
Helena:	Feel them as well.
?	Don't pull the grit off them.
Jesse:	Hands everywhere!
Daniel:	One at a time *
Jesse:	Quiet! [whisper]
Helena:	The lady or him might be thinking –

Daniel: Some of them look very sad don't they?
             [hubbub]
Jesse: That lady, they might be her babies.
Justin: Her head looks like an acorn a little bit, doesn't it? Her hat looks
             like an acorn
Helena: Yeh . . . her head looks like an acorn.

The acorn simile is in fact very apt, and Helen helpfully reinforces it.

Justin: And – and – anybody say anything else?
             [hubbub]
Jesse: I don't know what to talk.
?   Just get on with it. Just shut up [very roughly spoken; this is quite
             distressing for someone, I'd guess]
Justin: There's an eye here broken. There's an eye here what's broken.
Daniel: ***** fishtails.
Justin: So's that eye!
Helena or Jesse: Yeh looks a bit like a fish*tank*.
             [silence]
             [hubbub]
Justin: I know what that is! [shouting]
?   It's probably a fish probably or half a fishtail.
Jesse: How can it be? [scornful] They wouldn't have any, sort of, holes in!
Helena: Look at that face.
?   Don't hit, Justin.
?   Shhh!
?   She looks a bit happy don't she.
?   Well yeh!
Jesse: Maybe she's a teacher sort of and er, er these are all her children in
             her school
             [yell, response to thump, I suspect]
Jesse: I've just found out everything, I know, she's angry because they keep
             coming round, to get her.

Jesse makes it clear again that the children see the exercise as a kind of examination.

Helena: I know. She's angry because she doesn't want them climbing on her.
             [hubbub; 'very wooden' emerges out of it]
?   Justin!
Justin: Can we just get on with it, just get on with it, we're being taped
             [desperation] . . . You know this bit it's all a bit rough and a bit
             holey . . . when you slide your hand round this bit. It hurts a bit
             dunnit?

Helena: Nobody's talked about this bit have they? Nah not even the four
          under it!
Jesse: There is no writing under it!
          I'm sorry
Daniel: I've got it!
?   Shhhh! This is someone who is an artist
?   a famous artist and he's made something
Daniel: a famous artist, this is a famous artist and he's dead, right.
?   How do you know that?
Daniel: I've been to Egypt.
Helena: I know what it is . . . she or he –
Jesse: QUIET! QUIET! QUIET!
Helena: This is a famous artist and these are all dead now.

[Other children appear at the window: shoo! shoo! We appear and stop it, and
the children return to 'famous person', etc.]

Duncan, the headteacher, wrote to me about this tape, saying that the
Dictaphone had inhibited the children. Indeed, recording equipment always
contaminates talk. But there is no such thing as 'natural' (perhaps a better
word might be 'neutral') conversation in schools, untainted by external influences. As soon as we have language to manipulate each other with we aren't
'natural'. Language makes human beings human, and thereby infects them
with bias, and the presence of the machine recording that language is merely
an obvious, emblematic example. Other less evident ones are the teacher's
presence, visits by other adults, such as parents, students and, especially,
inspectors, and the social make-up of the group.

Absence of a teacher affects talk too, as we can see here, as children
hurriedly (and brutally) negotiate and adopt (and adapt) the roles they are
going to play:

> Everyone look at this all right and no talking about this. I'll start off,
> right cos – . . . All right, all right, let's get this done cos these people
> here . . . I'm the youngest! All right, Daniel; all right.

All talk is prey to viruses. Meeting someone new alongside an old friend
contaminates our usual frankness. Duncan is right to suggest, though, that
I'm not researching the children, but the children affected by the tape, just as
OFSTED inspectors are inspecting schools only as affected by their presence.

Duncan also says in his note that the tape exposes issues of peer group
relationships. It's about dominance, panic and withdrawal. The child (Duncan
says) with the most sophisticated language, Thomas, contributes almost
nothing. Daniel 'establishes the role of leader quickly and forcibly. He is a
bright, astute and confident child who, when in the company of adults, is
perhaps a trifle too eager to please. Very interesting to see how he reacts away

from adult eyes.' Daniel's domineering behaviour ('I'm the youngest! . . . Shhhhh!') could be said to be learnt from, in part, or encouraged by, my own behaviour at the beginning, which can stand for the language of teachers from time immemorial: 'Hang on a minute. Hang on a minute. What's your name?' Jesse and Justin occasionally panic.

Listening to this tape, I wonder if we as teachers don't teach much of the bullying language in the way we talk to children. I heard, for example, in another school: 'Into the hall now when I say, not before . . . NOW! In a row, along my arm, you're not straight, Mark, back! NOW! SIT!' This is, admittedly an extreme example of the Barbara Woodhouse method of organising children for assembly. But I believe most of us, as teachers, would be shocked by unedited transcripts of our talk with children, and one of the reasons would be that we exhibit the kind of peremptory (at best) and bullying (at worst) behaviour that we deplore in children.

Duncan said about Justin that he is 'the ostrich who puts the rest to flight'. Certainly, he contributes little to the unsupervised session apart from characteristic rising panic. While this may be a significant part of his make-up, I must take responsibility for some of this panic, because if a child is predisposed this way, the situation I presented him with (especially after I left the room) is only going to encourage such inclinations and behaviour. The learning for me here is that I must reassure the children that they are not being tested; perhaps to be completely open about what I am doing. It is typical of the times we live in that any new situation in schools is likely to be interpreted by both children and teachers as a testing situation.

The tape was, like the drowned father in *The Tempest*'s 'Full Fathom Five', 'something rich and strange'. In other words, it was everything a tape of children talking will be if we give them a chance. It shows many examples of children showing what they do know, and what they are learning as they think and talk. They are aware, from the beginning, as Duncan says, of the existence of another culture ('Egypt') though they did not comment on the Negro features of the carving.

The children are also, interestingly, aware of a function of art to commemorate. Daniel, for example, says, early on

> from when er somebody died they put their, some, person that they made it, they made a wood thing and they said it was a person

and Helena (who never lets herself be blown off track) immediately picks this up from Daniel:

> If they found a person that's dead, and they might have made, laid it down and then made a statue of it . . . That might be a famous person, so they put it in wood . . . and gave one to all the people in Egypt.

What I find depressing about this part of the transcript (and, indeed, about much else) is nothing to do with the children's talk, but the fact that I did not allow either Daniel or Helena to develop this theme. 'Thank you Daniel. Justin . . .' I say like a talk show host, on the first occasion and, on the second, generalising to the far less interesting Egypt idea. Why did I do this? Obviously it was not intentional. I suspect *I did not even notice the commemoration idea arising.* And this leads to the huge question: How much do we actually listen to children? How much attention do we pay them? We are all, as teachers, skilled in the social display of listening; we know about eye contact, about using a quieter voice that doesn't drown out the children's voices emotionally, and we know about making 'interested' noises at the end of what they say. But the evidence here is that I, at least, simply wasn't listening. And this, of course, breaks all Wells' principles. I have paid insufficient attention, I have not tried to understand, I have therefore been unable to take both the child's meaning as a basis for what to say next, nor to take account of the child's ability to understand. In the tapes of Alastair at home, by contrast, my attention to the boy's speech has been total.

A similar thing happens minutes later, when Jesse and Helena bring up the matter of death. They are thinking of starvation, thoughts coming, probably, from television pictures of the Rwandan war. I am interested in children talking about death generally – but as soon as I realise their agenda is different from mine, I lose interest. My 'Mmmmm' sounds dismissive. I move on to Daniel and, then, another subject. One might say, yet another subject.

The children produce, under the pressure of the situation, and of my relentless, shifting questioning, some beautiful images:

> a famous person . . . put in wood . . . trembling . . . scattering all around her . . . like a ladder . . . a chipper . . . the edge of it and chip the rest out (a perfect description, as Duncan says, of the way a chisel works) . . . her head looks like an acorn.

When my friend Helen Arnold read the transcript of the conversation about the carving of the African lady, she made the point that, though the talk was about a tangible object that was there, that they could look at and feel, the hypotheses they made about it were abstract, involving reasoning and thinking about the past; therefore the talk was disembodied.

Some science in the nursery

Finally, an example of nursery children talking about science. Their teacher, my wife Dawn, had filled balloons with water, shown them to the children, and then frozen them overnight in the freezer. We put them in the sink in the classroom and the children played with them, feeling, stroking, digging, watching, talking. We collected words they said, and told them they'd made a poem about the balloons, with our help. The result showed that four year olds can make metaphors and use resonant words; that they have a natural facility for alliteration; that they are apprentice poets. The poem said

An experiment in the nursery

Miss filled balloons with water
and we held them,
squeezy, slippery things.
soggy and squidgy.

She put them in the freezer.

When she took them out next day
the rubber split and peeled off
and we felt them again,

cold,

rock hard,
freezing things,
smooth,
slippery,
melty on the outside.

We looked closely
through a magnifying glass and saw

small windows on the ice
rainbow bubbles bubbling and popping
and lines inside
and lights.

They looked like moons
and they melted in our hands.

3

QUESTIONS

Children and moral issues

In this chapter I show children working with important moral issues, including anger and death.

My wife Dawn asked her five year olds about questions. She said, 'I want you to think of some questions you'd like to know the answers to but you don't think you ever will.' When I do this, as I have often, I repeat that several times very slowly, varying it slightly: 'What would you love to know about, but you think no book or person will ever be able to teach you about it? . . . What will you always, probably, be ignorant of?' When Dawn had collected a bundle of questions, she asked the children which question would they prefer to have repeated several times – at the end of each stanza of what was to become a poem, in fact.

Why do you get older when it's your birthday?
Why have people got names?
How do people talk
And how does the sun light up?

How does the river move?
Why are beaches by the sea?
Why are there millions of stones by the beach
And how does the sun light up?

How does chicken pox come?
Why do babies cry?
Why does Dad fight with Mum
And how does the sun light up?

How come wild animals are not in the street?
How does your heart get inside you?
Is God inside your body
And how does the sun light up?

45

How can the sun rise when you're asleep?
How does the moon follow you when you're in the car?
Does the sun go into the ground at night?
And how does the sun light up?

These questions came from a group of sixty seven-year-old children:

Why do tvs have tv screens?
Do cats dream?
Why do grown-ups fight all the time?
What made the world grow?
Why does Mummy go out all the time?
Why do grown-ups have power over children when children do not
have power over grown-ups?
Why do people grow?
How do you grow up?
Who made the church?
Why are mountains always slippery?
How do you get up in Heaven?
How does gravity hold you down?
How did God get made?
How are there different countries?
Why do teenagers get spots?
Why does my Dad look like a gorilla?
How did the sea get blue?
Why are girls clumsy?
Why do babies cry?
Why does beer make you drunk?
Why do fish make bubbles?
Why do daddies have bristles?
How does the sea suck you away?

I dealt with this differently, leaving the polished look of a poem for another
time. What do these questions teach us about children and their thinking –
assuming we are patient and respectful enough to listen and to pay attention?
The children are interested in disquieting moral issues:

Why do grown-ups fight all the time?
Why does Mummy go out all the time?
Why do grown-ups have power over children when children do not
have power over grown-ups?

They raise religious issues. This has happened in nearly every school where I
have led this activity:

Who made the church?
How do you get up in Heaven?
How did God get made?

Growth, understandably, interests the children:

What made the world grow?
Why do people grow?
How do you grow up?

The first session with these children ended with the disquieting question 'How does the sea suck you away?' Later the children wrote further questions. A group of five- to seven-year-old children contributed the following to my now large file of questions:

Why do octopuses have tentacles?
Why do people die?
Why are people born?
How did God get magic?
How does God move the furniture?
How did God come into the world without getting born?
What does God look like?
Is Jesus bald?
How do we know if a man is married or not?
Why do leaves fall off the trees?
How did Jesus come back to life when He hung on a cross?
How was the first man born when there was no one to have a baby?
How do we know if a man is horrible or not?
How do we know if God is true or not?

Religion is there, again, with worries about the truth or otherwise of belief, but also, bathetically, concerns about the appearance of Jesus, and whether God is a poltergeist. One question mirrors a central question in John's Gospel: How can a man be born again when he is old? Can he enter a second time into his mother's womb, and be born? (John 3:4) Other questions, notably 'How do we know if a man is horrible or not?', touch on areas of deep concern not only for children, but also for their parents. One can only speculate at what is going on in this girl's mind as she talks to a stranger in her school (me). In another school, one child put forward 'Why did my sister have to die?' and another, moments later, said, 'Why do aliens have longer half terms than us?' This strange jumping nature of the question sequence is significant. It is the way life is.

Unspoken language

What about unspoken language? A behaviourist would ignore this, because such behaviour is unobservable. But look at the drawing by four-year-old Lauren in her school nursery (Illustration 7). Her teacher tells me that she is not a talkative child. On the day she made this picture, her mother had been taken into hospital. We do not need to know the unknowable (what words were going through this child's mind as she made this image) but we do need to understand that there were words; and that the words were of significance in terms of at least two important aspects of her life: her development as a thinker, talker and writer, and her suffering as her mother left her, however temporarily. All that space around the main image, which we might once have cut off for the sake of neatness and saving space on the wall, we now know is part of the picture, a place for thought and feeling and disturbed speculation. Thus, generally, we can look with greater interest at children's drawings and interpret them in terms of their thinking and talking and writing.

Children thinking and talking about anger

Children talk with passion about moral and allied issues unless, for some reason, they are prevented from doing so. And they sometimes are!

Child to teacher on duty: Henry hit me, Miss.
Teacher: Oh, I'm sure he didn't.

One of the most potent ways of opening issues to do with right and wrong is to explore anger as a class. Beth is teaching her six year olds on the carpet in the corner of the room. She asks, 'What makes you angry?' and the answers come thick and fast. Then she asks, 'What do you do when you're angry? . . . How do you feel?' Again, the response is strong. Later, she typed up the children's sentences (her helper had been noting down what the children said) and printed them on drawings the children did of their angry faces:

> When I'm angry I feel sad, red and mad as blood, red as a rose, red as tomato sauce. I am angry when my friends aren't kind to me, I am angry when my sister hits me on the head, or my brother keeps beating me up. I get angry when my Grandad teases me.

> When I'm cross I scream . . . I stamp my foot on my bed . . . I cry . . . I shout at people . . . I want to be on my own . . . I feel red and mad inside . . . I show my teeth . . . I throw my toys . . . I play by myself . . . I run to my room . . . I sit on the settee and I won't eat or drink . . . I throw things . . . I get hot.

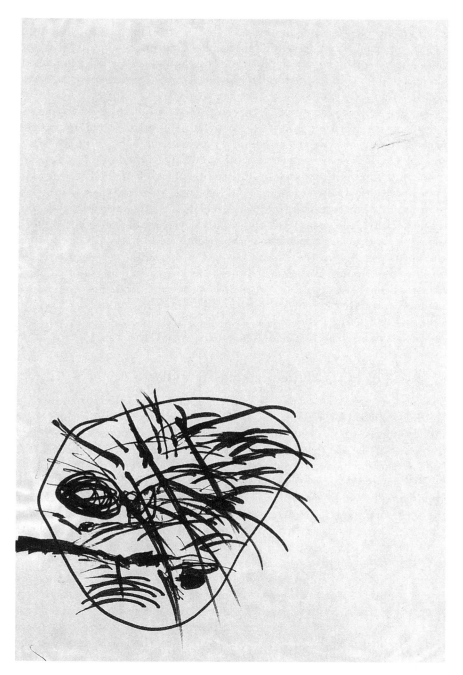

Illustration 7

Beth had here provoked similes and metaphors ('red as tomato sauce', for example) by questions, or unfinished phrases: 'red like . . .' and leaving a silence pregnant with a potential answer hanging in the air. Also, she had asked them a question that sounds strange to some adults, perhaps, but which has meaning for children, and which provokes immediate and vivid responses: 'What colour are you inside when you are angry?'

As they draw, children release the possibility of talk. Somehow, concentration on the mechanical activity of moving the graphic tool around the paper in response to whatever stimulus provokes another part of the brain, and the children delve energetically for words. The other examples here are from children in different schools. Illustrations 8 and 9 are by five year olds. Note how they have been encouraged to write, and then read their writing out to an adult, who has transcribed it underneath. This then becomes a reading lesson for the child, who reads the standard version of her words back to the adult, and then, probably, to another adult and to a group of children; and then, possibly, to the whole class. All this reading experience would be lost if the children were not allowed (as they aren't in Stalin Country Primary School: see pp. 123–5) to write words down until they could spell them properly. And experience leads to the kind of free and easy writing in Illustrations 10–12.

There is more about these children and anger in Chapter 6.

Children talking about death

Two groups of people – writers of the Book of Common Prayer and young children – know that, when it comes to honest writing, niceness doesn't come into it: 'In the midst of life we are in death', wrote Cranmer's team, and a five-year-old girl said to her teacher: 'My Great-Auntie died not long ago. She had a stroke and died in the hospital.'

The classroom unmentionable is not sex. It is death. Yet very young children reflect readily on what faces them: their grandparents almost always, their parents sometimes, their brothers and sisters now and then, die. Children have chanted its reality on the playground: 'Old Abram Brown is dead and gone/You'll never see him more'. They know it'll be their reality one day. Fortunate children, weeping over the hamster's tiny corpse, or a cat's memorial in the garden, see death first in their pets. If this doesn't happen at home, it must happen in classrooms. Our love of animals offers the safest way of ensuring that this issue is faced. I watched a teacher read a class of ten year olds a short poem about the death of a rabbit. She pointed out that the poem had a repeated line; that it ended as it had begun, the last line echoing the first. She asked the children to write 'short poems about pets you loved that had died. Perhaps you could put some of these things in it: a phrase someone used about it – maybe something one of your parents used to say; a repetition; some memories; a description'.

Illustration 8

Illustration 9

Charlotte Towse 7

I hated it When my nan and Grandad took me to the beach I did not like it I throuing a Paddie I Went red on my face and I Went near the rowing boat and I felt sad I didn't Want to go to the beach

Illustration 10

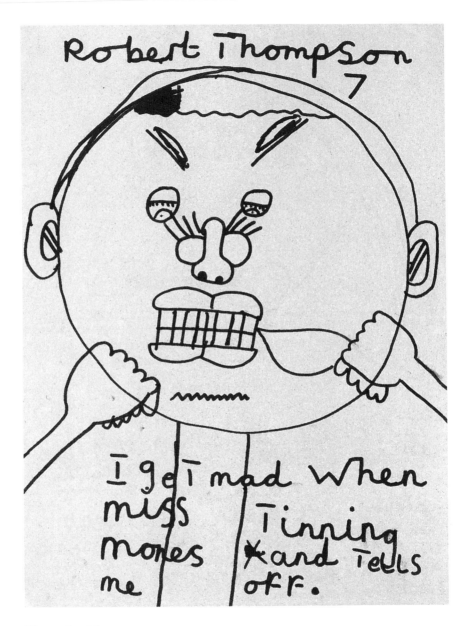

Illustration 11

Illustration 12

55

Natter usually went before writing in this classroom. But now there was silence. An Emily Dickinson poem says: 'I like a look of agony/Because I know it's true'. Michelle found, after the death of her rabbit, that everything was 'as quiet as a deer'. Danielle remembered how her father used to say that the ducklings that her pet duck had produced 'looked like little tulips'. The spark that writing makes fly between children and dead animals is the most powerful of connections in learning, first because death is such a powerful subject, and second because the spark flies with love. This writing changes the child, and education is essentially about change.

Children face large scary facts, and the deaths of animals help them to practise coping with them. Deaths of animals are dreadful. But then, their loved humans, givers of presents, wrinkled sitters in chairs, old walkers . . . they disappear, too, as the animals do. A five year old said to my wife:

> My Great-Auntie died not long ago. She had a stroke and died in the hospital. She had white hair. She was my Daddy's Auntie. My Dad's got a headache now. She had glasses. The hospital took her jewellery off. So when the girls in our family get married they can wear her jewellery – that's me and my cousins.
>
> I have got a bracelet with crystals and a wedding ring. It is silver.
>
> She lived in a flat in London. She used to give me pork pie and chocolate biscuits and cups of tea. Sometimes I cry at home about her. It's sad when somebody dies. She's up in Heaven now and she can see us writing this. But we can't see her.
>
> My Mum cried in the funeral taxi.

This really is the truthful look of agony. And it is what we are preparing children for when they write about Tiffany and Coco.

Finally, a bridge across to the writing section of my book, and across to older students. A fifteen year old, Sarah Fisher, writes with disturbing detachment. This book is about young children, but this poem is useful in reminding us that our infants grow and change, and that the richness they show us at five, six and seven develops into a different richness in the junior and secondary years:

Departure

The room is dark.
The curtains have been drawn,
The doors closed.
On the dresser, the flowers begin to wilt.

The bed is filthy
But not worth changing now
And the figure in it cannot be moved.

One arm lies on the tide-marked duvet.
It is motionless.
When the doctor lifted it
The skin hung underneath like
Her bracelets used to.

The skin of the face is waxy and shiny
In contrast to the pillows.
It is yellow, and the veins can be seen
Pumping slowly, full of clots.

Around the corners of the mouth
Are little circles of dried liquid
And the lips are shrivelled and brittle.

The eyelids are only thin stretched of membrane.
The sockets are outlined clearly in gray mottled flesh.
Her hair has fallen out.
Only one eyelash clings beneath the closed lids.

The room grows darker.
It is 6 p.m. in November
And downstairs
The floors creak.
In another half-hour
There will be a muted relative by the bedside
Praying.

With a flutter
The floral curtains
Billow in the softest of breezes.

We'll be there, one day. And Sarah is the healthier for having rehearsed her feelings now, as she writes, and for not colluding in what Philip Larkin calls 'the costly aversion of the eyes from death'. And the other children quoted here too, young as they are, are all the richer for having confronted the last enemy.

AN INTERLUDE

CHILDREN MAKING THEIR
OWN BOOKS

In this interlude, I suggest a way of making an anthology of children's rhymes that might engage both adults and children in the infant classroom; later I suggest that children making their own books for each other is a purposeful way of exploring various issues in literacy. In between these two items, there are some poems composed by very young children, in various languages.

If one sees reading as 'a process of building up from individual words, to individual letters, to sentences, in a neat hierarchical progression' (Styles and Drummond 1993 – their description of a view they deplore) the thought of children reading their own books will be illogical to say the least. Thinkers about children and literacy who conceive of learning in such neat, unrealistic terms will see such a notion as nonsense. They would ask questions like: How could they monitor the books children write, and who has read them? How could they make sure that children, in writing their books, use only the letters the other children (who are going to read their books) can cope phonetically with? How will they ensure that the children learn about letters and sounds in the right order? How, above all, will they keep control of the children's learning? Orderly, cautious, uncreative, essentially social trainers rather than educators, these people will place such practice, with much else, in inverted commas and call it 'progressive' and

> a hydra-headed beast named real books/ storybook method/ emergent reading/ holistic approach/ osmosis/ apprenticeship approach . . . led by hot gospellers, livid with intolerant enthusiasm . . . with evangelical zeal.
>
> (Martin Turner, quoted in Styles and Drummond 1993)

I have never heard anyone claim that children learn to read by 'osmosis'. This word, representing a parody of a position, has been allowed to become, absurdly, a neutral description of that position. And how do those who 'don't believe in emergent readers' (as the deputy headteacher of Stalin County Primary put it to me) see children. If they are not 'emergent' readers, are they the opposite? 'Retiring', perhaps, or 'withdrawing' readers? If they are emergent runners, musicians, philosophers, horse riders and nurses, why aren't they emergent readers? The language that Turner uses is evidence of intemperate anger at two things. First, he is angry because the idea of children 'emerging' as readers (and writers) chips at the phonic/remedial deficit model that he sets so much store by. And second, he is angry because he senses some of his control of children's literacy passing to the children themselves.

These two paragraphs may look as though they should be in Part III. But reading and writing are arguably more intimate with each other than any other two intellectual human activities are, and to treat children with the respect they are due seems to require us to understand them as both emergent readers and emergent writers in the same breath. What follows are examples of children reading, first, what they have compiled, and second, what they have written.

Playground rhymes and their significance

Children are collectors. They love to make anthologies. Elizabeth Grugeon (1988) reintroduces us to an old friend of many teachers, and of other people working with children: the playground rhyme. Anthologies of these verses are exhilarating reads. There are many useful books and articles containing vigorous examples: Walter (1989), Rosen and Steele (1990), Shaw (1970) and the standard, and irreplaceable, works by the Opies (1959, 1988). Agard and Nichols (1991) offer examples from the Caribbean, as does Hallworth (1994).

Grugeon overheard a young child clapping with an older friend. They were saying

> Batman and Robin in the batmobile,
> Batman did a fart and paralysed the wheel,
> The car wouldn't go, the engine wouldn't start,
> All because of Batman and his supersonic fart.

Grugeon comments: 'I was impressed. At five and six weeks in school, "supersonic" and "paralysed" were not part of her daily discourse.' They rarely appear during the literacy hour. As she implies, school steals this language from the children, and replaces it with 'Roger ran' and 'Jennifer went out', the language to which writers like Martin Turner (quoted in Styles and Drummond 1993) would restrict all young learners. Outside Turner's control, on the other hand, the children's language is lively and multi-syllabic. The vigour of crude slapstick wit, as well as the sophistication of longer words, is there in the children's playground talk, but not in any of their talk or writing in the classroom. When teachers talk of 'success' or 'failure' in language, they are never discussing underground knowledge and rites. They are merely discussing the one limited language they have left with the child. It is as though accomplished poets were to be assessed day by day on their punctuation, or skilled footballers on their adeptness at thumping the ball over the stand, or ballet dancers on their ability to stand up straight on tiptoe.

I have been collecting unsystematically rhymes from playgrounds in Britain for many years, as has Grugeon. Some of these rhymes are for counting out to see who will be 'it'. Children say others while they clap hands in pairs or even in threesomes: always, it has to be said, they are girls. Other rhymes are satirical squibs at the expense of people in authority – teachers, especially. I have learned, like other collectors before me, that what children 'learn from each other' has the life of the truly vital. It is living poetry. I have written about some of this material with my wife (Sedgwick and Sedgwick 1996). What follows are rhymes I have collected from children in Hertfordshire, Suffolk, Durham, Berkshire, Norfolk and other counties, and placed in a book and given back to children for their comments. I have done this in the belief that the power of poetry begins not with the first verses children learn in classrooms but with the rhymes they say for various purposes on playgrounds. It will be unfortunate if the current trend in many schools to reduce the length of playtime (to help prevent bullying, save on staff costs or make room for more of the National Curriculum) also curtails children's opportunities to learn the playground rhymes. Iona and Peter Opie comment in *The Lore and Language of Schoolchildren*:

> The scraps of lore which children learn from each other are at once more real, more immediately serviceable, and more vastly entertaining to them than anything which they learn from grown-ups.
>
> (Opie and Opie 1959)

Some of these rhymes are very ancient, and when we say them we are momentarily in touch with our deepest roots. 'Eeny meeni miny mo' comes from ancient ways of counting. Compare it with old numbers like these:

> een, teen, tuther, futher, fip, soother, loader, porter, dubber, dick, een dick, teen dick, tuther dick, futher dick, bumpit, een bumpit, teen bumpit, tuther bumpit, futher bumpit, gig it

which is the way the first twenty pages of Geoffrey Summerfield's (1970) wonderful (but now out of print) anthology *Junior Voices The First Book* are numbered.

Other rhymes have links with ancient charms and secret passwords. 'Ocka pocka dominocka', which exists in many countries in variations such as

63

'Hocca proach domma noach', can be traced to the moment in the Mass when the priest holds high the Host and says the words of Christ at the Last Supper: 'Hoc est enim corpus meum' ('This is my body'). This solemnity is yoked to childish practice in a story told years ago on television by an adult who had heard children playing funerals. One of them said: 'In the name of the Father, the Son, and in the hole he goes'. None of this is necessarily irreverent. Children know that elements of life, however serious, seen without a sense of the incipiently ridiculous, are only half-seen. Many of these rhymes link children from all over the world in their laughter. For this reason alone, if for no other, they are to be treasured. They bind together all members of the largest and most innocent of savage tribes, the young.

Many of the rhymes, of course, are about love. Here's one such:

Matthew and Kimberley
sitting in a tree
K – I – S – S – I – N – G.
First comes love,
then comes marriage,
then comes a baby
in a baby-carriage.

Children have told me that they like this one for two reasons. The first is 'because it rhymes': they sense this, but can rarely identify the 'ley – tree – G' rhyme. The second reason is 'because it is funny'. They said both those things about the following, which I found in a US Air Force Base school in Norfolk:

Miss Mary Mack

Miss Mary Mack Mack Mack
all dressed in black black black
with silver buttons buttons buttons
all down her back back back.

She asked her mother mother mother
for fifty cents cents cents
to see the elephant elephant elephant
jump the fence fence fence.
He jumped so high high high
He reached the sky sky sky
and didn't come back back back
till the fourth of July – ly – ly.

The repetitions were very important to all the children who commented on this one. The next rhyme shows how children are very casual in their appreciation of rhyme. 'Jupiter/stupider', for example, and 'Pepsi/sexy':

Boys are rotten,
made out of cotton,
girls are handy,
made out of candy,
boys go to Jupiter,
to get more stupider,
girls go to college
to get more knowledge,
boys drink whisky
to get more frisky,
girls drink Pepsi
to get more sexy.

A reservation about using children's rhymes in school

Naturally, speakers of these rhymes are not too particular about grammar ('more stupider'). But only the most churlish adult would correct them. They show us the beginnings of adult realities: love and quarrelling, for example, and stupid men drinking whisky, and women in pubs with them sipping colas. And sex is often on the edge of things ('show my knickers to the football team'). Despite this, one child's comments on the following rhyme was enlightening:

Teacher, teacher I declare
Let me see your underwear.
Is it black or is it white?
Oh my Gosh it's dynamite.

The child assumed, wrongly I think, that the rhyme had been written for children by an adult, and she said, 'I don't like that, it's rude [long hesitation] ... people write rude things like that 'cos they think children'll like them, but they don't'. When this six-year-old girl said this, the other four children round the table burst into a chorus of agreement.

This led me to reflect on some poetry published for children. There is a kind of book – typically very thin, on cheap paper, with a low price (usually a dubious penny below three or four pounds) that is stocked in part with 'pee po belly bum drawers' material 'because it sells' – or so editors and publishers frequently tell me. But these children were adamant that they did not like this sort of verse. I wonder why? It is, I suspect, an invasion of their privacy, not of their individual privacy, but of their tribe's. Children talk on the playground about sex because they sense (at first) then know (later) it is important. They know this partly because children come trailing those clouds of glory to which I've referred before, and partly because they've noticed that the adult world – through television, through newspapers, through films, through hidden, half-hidden and non-hidden conversations, behaves as if these things were important. They, therefore, want to learn. They want to know. They are subject to a basic fear of misunderstanding something that both their instinct and their society tells them is (in a pristine sense of the word) vital. To have adults (as they see it) make up 'rude' verses for them is to have the process of learning short-circuited; it is to be patronised.

Connected with this reason is another one: children do not like vulgarity in Coleridge's sense ('The ignorant . . . and sordid vulgarity of the leaders of the day') nearly as much as we think they like it. And if these books sell it is not because children buy them, but because adults do. I have a poem in one of these publications. When I tell children the title of the book – *Snoggers* – they groan and yeuggh and squirm. They know deep inside themselves that in poetry we do infinitely more than gain laughs at the expense of ourselves and our sexuality. They know that we tap the life blood of our culture and hear the primal rhythms of our existence. Whether the poem is a rhyme sung at a football match, or an exploration of the silence, leading to reflection, or meditation, on our loves, hates and terrors, it is basic to our very nature. It combines our sense of the rhythms of life: heartbeat, normal, excited, in love, in distress; walking pace, running pace; the rhythms of our hours, days, weeks, months and years. It links all this with something else that is quintessentially poetic: the search for the centre; what is there in each of us, at the beginning at least, that wants to know, that veers away from the sham and the sentimental.

Marian Whitehead (1993) cautions us to reflect on what we do when we take over nursery rhymes as part of a strategy for teaching children to read. There is, she says, in this a 'possible under-valuing of the other things that nursery rhymes do (apart from supporting phonological awareness)'. These rhymes are often subversive, and we should not '[pull] the carnivalesque and subversive elements of the oral tradition into the orbit of formal school reading instruction'. The same applies to playground rhymes, some of which Whitehead quotes, admiring their realism as well as their subversive nature:

> I wish I wuz a seagull,
> I wish I wuz a duck,
> So I could fly along the beach
> And watch . . .
>
> (Lurie 1990, quoted in Whitehead 1993)

and

> Fudge fudge tell the judge
> Mama had a baby,
> It's a boy full of joy,

Papa's going crazy.
Wrap it up in toilet paper,
Send it down the elevator.

(Lurie 1990, quoted in Whitehead 1993)

Whenever we use playground rhymes in classrooms, we should remember
who they belong to; we should not hi-jack them into reading schemes, or
other material for controlling children's reading. And we should not misuse
them, or patronise the children, by imitating those rhymes in our own poems.
We may, though, invite children to compile their own books of rhymes, and
ask them to perform them, read them, alter them, discuss them or use them
in any ways they think appropriate.

Poems by very young children

Interesting examples of very young children from all over the world
composing poems have been published in *Montessori Education*: Ann Dowker
(1996), of the Department of Experimental Psychology at Oxford University,
helped young children to make poems. She began with 133 children aged
between two and six years in nursery centres and a primary school in London.
The researchers showed children various pictures (a playground, a night-time
scene, a forest, a snowy day) and various images (a cat, a bird, a horse, a fish).
They then asked the children to tell a story about each picture, and played the
story back to them on a tape recorder. Each researcher told the children that
she was going to tell them a poem 'which is a bit like a story but not quite'
and that she would like them to make up something like that.

Dowker's definition of a poem was very basic and, like all such attempts,
contentious: it was, for her, 'any production which had an obvious rhythmical
structure'. 'A bit like a story but not quite' begs a few questions as well for the
same generic reasons. Setting aside for another time and place the arguments
about this definition, which is, to say the least, simplistic and behaviourist,
we must recognise straightaway that Dowker's technique produced
interesting rhyming verbal constructs from children 'among all social classes
and even [*sic*] from those with very limited English'. I include these poems
here, with a commentary on them, because they are different from the usual
conception of poetry by children which has sprung from the creative writing
movement and writers like James Reeves, David Holbrook and Sandy
Brownjohn. I discuss such poems at some length in my own book (Sedgwick
1997a).

Genevieve was four when she composed this:

There was a little horse in
Bowhinney Lane
Don't take him for a ride again.

Note how this rhyme uses a local name, as many poems for children do; see traditional rhymes and Charles Causley's (1996) work for children. Naming places is also a feature of mainstream poetry: see especially Edward Thomas. His 'What shall I give my daughter the younger' and 'If I were to own this countryside' are examples of the Adam- and Eve-like naming function that poets, above all artists, have. Returning to Genevieve's poem, note also the way it implies, between 'Lane' and 'don't', something appalling that has happened that we can only guess at, so that the adult needs, upon repetition and reflection, to supply another line in there:

> There was a little horse in
> Bowhinney Lane.
> He ran away to Scotland, O
> Don't take him for a ride again.

But perhaps the most exciting of Dowker's examples came when fellow-researchers applied the same techniques to Italian, French, Polish and Brazilian children. Here is an Italian girl aged 4.11:

(1)

> C'era una volta
> Pero Sevolta
> Casca la topa
> Pero se copa.

I am going to withhold the translations of these poems because I think that non-Italian speakers can gain something from these words without knowing what they mean. Say the poem aloud, and you get some idea of not only what this child was saying, but also what she inherits from her tradition.

Here is a French poem by a boy age six years:

(2)

> Martin le papin
> Courait dans le jardin

An Italian poem by a boy aged four and a half – note here the powerful alliteration:

(3)

> Una volta una volpe voleva voltare.

A six year old French boy:

(4)

> Le cochon est gros comme une armoire.

This example is interesting because of its use of a comparison.

Finally, a Brazilian girl aged five years five months:

(5)

> O gatinho e branquinho como nuvem.
> O gatinho e branquinho como e papel.
> O gatinho gost de jogar bolinha e come.
> Lette feito un bebe.

Translations:

(1)

> Once upon a time there was
> Pero Sevolta.
> The mouse fell
> Pero killed himself.

(2)

> Martin the rabbit
> ran in the garden.

(3)

> Once upon a time a fox wanted to fly.

(4)

> The pig is as fat as a wardrobe.

(5)

> The kitten is white as clouds.
> The kitten is white as paper.
> The kitten likes to play with a ball, and drinks
> Milk like a baby.

Children making their own books

In order to live, a society must create a literature. It must have a law, in the widest sense of teaching, guidance and revelation, as well as in the narrow one of rules and sanctions. It must have speeches, hymns and celebrations. It must have epics and sagas and prophecy, and ribaldry and folk songs and children's rhymes. It must have stories about its history, some accepting, some sceptical. It must have a poetry that attempts to tell the truth about the world that is to come; that attempts more than the usual feeling with more than the usual form, none simply accepting of the ways things are or seem to be, but all at least initially sceptical. Without all this language, as without vision, a society perishes.

69

One example out of many of a society's necessary literature is the Old Testament: the essential teaching in the first five books, the poetry in the Psalms, Proverbs, Lamentations and elsewhere; the history in Judges and Samuel among other books. The more than usual feeling combined with the more than usual form can be seen most clearly in Psalm 119, where each of 22 sections begins with a Hebrew letter, and each verse in each section begins with the same letter: the whole a deeply felt poem. One can find such literature in every culture in the world. Because of all these imperatives, language, and in particular writing, is the central element in schools in any society, whether it is acknowledged as such or not. So that society must honour the words of children, from the first 'Mama' or 'Dada' to the last word of an essay or a poem or a scientific dissertation or an examination of a dance. And since, in a vibrant society everyone will remain a student, the honouring must go beyond the end of schooling; it must last till the final mental note made in an old mind on a puzzling novel, poem or play.

One important aspect of inducting children into their necessary cultural tradition is helping them to know what books can do. We can demystify what books are by getting them to make their own.

Some of the best books for preparing children to be fluent readers are books they have written themselves. At Peartree Spring Infant school in Stevenage, children have been making their own books for some time. There are several reasons for the high quality of such books when compared to those made by publishers: the subject matter in these books is fascinating to the children, because they have chosen it; the difficulty level is right; the children are proud of something they have made, rather than puzzled or bored (possibly) by a commercial product; they have broken part of themselves off, and made it exist on its own, and that is a wonderful feeling, as all artists know. Also, the child's book doesn't cost anything! This idea is, of course, mentioned in the National Curriculum, and it is common practice in many classrooms.

I have in front of me a book now, made by six-year-old Oliver. Its construction is as follows: a sheet of A4 paper has been divided in half lengthways; this length of folded paper has been divided again into four small rectangles. The paper has then been made into a concertina shape. The front says

I used to be but now I am. Oliver Johnson

then there is a drawing of birds flying, a palm tree, stars and rocks. The next few pages read, with drawings alternating:

I used to go to church
But now I play on my Nintendo.

70

I used to be sick in the toilet
but now I'm sick in the sea.

I used to live on Saturn But now I live on the sun.

I used to be a dinosaur but now I'm a frog.

Some nursery children in another school made these texts:

I went to Cornwall

I went to Cornwall.
I stayed in a chalet.
It had a brown door
with number 55 on it.
There were bunk beds for kids.

I went to Cornwall.
I put my hands in the cold sea.
Stephen found some crabs' legs.
He nipped at me and Ashley.
The crabs' legs stinked so we put them in the bin.

I went to Cornwall.
Ashley and me went to Tiger Club.
Nicky and Gary looked after us there.
They said 'Where, where, where are we?'
We shouted, 'Tiger Club!'

Jo-Anne

Butterflies

I see butterflies in my garden.
Butterflies fly.
Sometimes they land on grass.
or on the soft ground
where there's no grass.

I see butterflies in my garden.
They look like moths.
Some are yellow and some are blue.
They have got long ears and a little head.

I see butterflies in my garden.
They have got two bug wings.
They swing their wings about
or wiggle them about.
That makes them fly.

I see butterflies in my garden.
If I was a butterfly
I'd fly to America
and find some grass to eat.
Then I'd fly back to Ipswich
and find my home.

Matthew

The teacher had asked Jo-Anne about her summer holiday, and had then written down quickly what she had said. The rest of the poem was provoked by further questioning ('What was your chalet like? What did you do at the camp?'). The teacher had then typed it out, and helped Jo-Anne to make it into a book. With this experience behind her, the child will inevitably understand and value books later in life. When Matthew said his piece, it was not during a writing session. He was painting outside during a warm autumn morning, and his poem stemmed from the painting. The teacher got her notebook 'dead quick' (as she put it to me later) and wrote his words down, and then, once again, provoked more words with further questions that can easily be inferred from Matthew's book.

The teacher read them back to the children, and they listened with eyes wide with pleasure. Then Jo-Anne read hers in part, to a visitor. Of course, she could read only some of the words: she read her book as one does a foreign newspaper on holiday, certain words springing out readily, others having to be inferred from context, others mentally noted for looking up later, yet others given up on.

Part II

CHILDREN AND WRITING

4

CHILDREN AND WRITING

Writing can do everything that language in general can do.

Frank Smith

Using the work of Frank Smith as a basis, this chapter attempts to demonstrate the importance of writing for learning, and places it in the context of humankind's earliest writing. Following Donald Graves (1983), it suggests that as teachers we all too often put unnecessary problems in the way of children writing.

In drafting and redrafting this section (and, eventually, in reluctantly and nervously letting it go) I am profoundly influenced by the work of Frank Smith. When I first read his book *Writing and the Writer* (1982), it became axiomatic immediately for me that 'Writing is a process of learning. We change as we write.' I suspect that before I had seen writing as a process by which I recorded what I had already learnt. Now I realised that I learned as I wrote. I amassed what to me was an impressive army, or at least platoon, of writers who felt the same as this, but who put it more succinctly and more elegantly: 'How can I tell what I think till I see what I say?'; 'You change as you write. You change yourself, you change the way you think'; 'How many of us in fact discover our convictions from what we write, instead of writing in obedience to known convictions?' These were my favourite sentences on this subject, from W. H. Auden, Doris Lessing and Geoffrey Grigson respectively. I formulated it myself, in my only attempt at an aphorism, like this: *Each poem is a research project into the difference between me and the rest of the world.*

Frank Smith says that his book is an act of learning as well as a communication of the already-learnt. This book, too, is a process of learning. It follows from the above that, contrary to what is probably the commonsense view, writers do not write a book because they know all about the subject, but because the fascination, the obsession with the subject of the book is so powerful that the writers want to know more. So they write.

75

Smith had wanted his book to be 'the record of its own odyssey'. This was impossible because it was like making a film about that particular film. Also, writing covers its own traces. The deletions, the furious pitching of screwed up paper into the bin, the papers discarded following the activity of an editing friend or (not, by any means necessarily the same thing) an editor – all that hides the process and prevents the writing being its own record. Writing, unlike speech, can be rearranged, and writers manipulate time and space. For example, Smith talks about what will happen later – though he has already written about what will happen later. This subject is full of paradoxes, and this is one of them: a text can rub its history out; but can look back into its own future.

Why write? Writing is relevant to all human experiences. Socially, we communicate with it, we keep records with it and it makes art. But its most significant value for those of us concerned with learning and teaching is its personal utility. What are the uses of language to the individual? What does language do?

- It gets our material needs met.
- It enables us to change other human beings' behaviour.
- It enables us to establish relationships with others.
- It enables us to express our perceptions of ourselves.
- It enables us to seek new knowledge.
- It enables us to exercise the imagination.
- It enables us to describe situations and ideas.
- It enables us to have fun.
- It enables us to establish agreement or expectations.
- It provides a record of the past.

(derived from Smith 1982)

The literate child

The English policy at Tacolneston School says about writing:

The Literate Child (who leaves our school at 8 years of age) should be able to

- Write confidently, without fear of making mistakes;
- Know where to go for help;
- Use strategies for self-evaluation, and self-correction;
- Write for a variety of purposes and for a range of audiences;
- Write with sustained concentration and appropriate pace;
- Operate as authors, using a range of secretarial skills.

Let us compare these aims with conventional (and, currently, political) wisdom about what actually happens, or should happen, in schools. We might, first, contrast that word 'confidently' with another word frequently used in this sort of document: 'correctly'. We might also note that 'without fear' and reflect on children in the middle of their SATs (standard assessment tasks). We might note that this school emphasises 'self-correction' and 'self-evaluation' rather than correction and evaluation by outside influences. We might note, too, those enriching words 'variety' and 'range' and contrast them with 'basic' and other words from the current rhetoric.

We might note the use of the word 'author', and reflect on the fact that, as Frank Smith says, totalitarian regimes need readers but discourage authors. Whitehead (1993) says:

> The imposition of such things as reading primers, anthologised extracts from 'great literature' and the speaking of standard English in schools are old and established features of education for docility.

The enforced reading of lifeless texts, along with the banning of creative literature, in both societies and in schools, are both aspects of control. Writing risks changing the world. See, for example, what writers in the former Soviet Union and in apartheid South Africa collectively achieved in helping people to understand and, indeed, change their predicament.

Early writing

What do we know about the early history of writing? It is worth digressing briefly in this area, because of the connections between, for example, cave drawings, and children's early marks. What we might call linguistic fossils date back no more than four or five thousand years. The Sumerians and Akkadians in Ancient Mesopotamia, between the Tigris and Euphrates rivers, developed symbols that represented aspects of the business of farmers and administrators of an agricultural economy: sacks of grain, heads of cattle and so on. Pictograms developed: mountains represented by simplified mountain shapes, woman by a pubic triangle – and then both symbols together denoted a woman from over the mountains, a foreign woman; thus, by extension, a slave (see Jean 1987 for a full and fascinating account of this).

But we can learn from drawings in caves more than fifteen thousand years old that human beings communicated with each other using drawings. These are not, Jean says, strictly writing, because writing has some elements of consistency and regularity. But these drawings are related to writing in that they both communicate. They are made by one human to tell another human something. Of course, what these drawings are about – what they are telling – is difficult, possibly impossible, to know. Are they practical? 'We have killed a bison.' Are they orders? 'Kill a bison, or else.' Are they religious, like the medieval wall paintings that have been uncovered in churches: terrible warnings about sin, or celebrations of and anxieties about the greatness of

77

God? Or are they art for the sake of art? Are they, in other words, examples of humankind rejoicing in an ability, a facility with lines, the pleasure they give, and the way they help us to evaluate and re-evaluate the world in which we find ourselves? Are they, to put it another way, play? 'The creative writer', Freud tells us, 'does the same as the child at play' (Vernon 1970:127). The same is true of every visual artist, too, at whatever point in pre-history or history he or she has flourished.

In Spain, a pregnant horse, twenty thousand years old, rears on its hind legs deep under the ground in the Pileta Caves, near Ronda in Andalusia; ancient already when King David thrived and someone wrote his psalms, a visual image older than 'The Lord is my Shepherd'. It makes my eyes, whenever I see it, prickle with tears. It teaches us about, if nothing else, the primacy of mark-making in humankind's life. If this is true for early humankind, it is also true for each human in his or her earliest years. Whenever I examine the horse, or my reflection on it, or my memory of it, for meaning, I learn again that, if I respect each child I teach, I will search the child's early marks for meaning too, and for evidence of those clouds of glory. I will constantly bear in mind those principles of Wells (see p. 21) about paying attention, and trying to understand, and using that understanding as a basis for what to say next to the child.

Here is the connection between those cave dwellers with their communications, and the children we teach with their marks. Those people wanted, needed, to communicate by drawings. Children want to communicate, to write (as well as draw). As Graves (1983) says:

> They want to write the first day they attend school . . . Before they went to school they marked up walls, pavements, newspapers with crayons, chalk, pens or pencils . . . The child's marks say, 'I am' . . . 'No, you aren't', say most school approaches to the teaching of writing. We ignore the child's urge to show what he knows . . . we take the control away from children and place unnecessary roadblocks in the way of their intentions. Then we say, 'They don't want to write. How can we motivate them?'

Graves was writing a long time ago, but what he says is still all too frequently true. A writer in an educational magazine asks 'What can I do to inspire some love of knowledge in my six-year-olds?' This is an example of a genre of facetiousness common in educational journalism, but this should not hide the fact that much schooling acts on the demonstrably false assumption that children are ignorant and unwilling to learn; that they are blank pieces of paper on which we must write, often against their will. The roadblocks we place in the way of children and their writing include making them copy our script; giving them examples of grammatically exemplary but imaginatively empty prose to read; and treating them as non-starters when they are already lovers, communicators, movers, survivors (see Sedgwick and Sedgwick 1996: 2–6).

We also block children's writing ourselves by treating writing as something only they do. In other words, as something that is done in schools only by the little people, by those without any power. If we were to write with children, how different the message would be. Graves (1983:43) has a trenchant page on this issue where he points out that children hardly ever see adults writing, and that they believe that when an adult does write, the words come by magic, 'Shazam!' It is our duty as teachers to disabuse children of this attractive fantasy. And the way to do it is to write with the children.

Beth, a teacher, said to me:

> I used to think – I said it often enough, and I'm ashamed of it now – I used to say that I had no time to write with the children. Now I keep a journal, a little notebook, where I write things down during the day. Anything – messages, shopping lists if I think of something I need to get for tea . . . sometimes I have a go at the poem or the story I've just asked them to write.

This notebook/journal approach is a good beginning, because it is un-threatening. Anybody can write what Beth showed me on one page, a shopping list, or, on another, a list of things that 'must get done' before Christmas. (This latter, by the way, led off with four clerical tasks demanded by the system in which she now works as a teacher, after which it modulated into humanity by mentioning the family for whom she had to buy presents.)

Later Beth became braver:

> The children were writing one day, and I could hardly concentrate on teaching because I'd had a row in the staffroom with [a colleague] at playtime, and I was so angry at what he'd been saying, it was sexist stuff, oh you can imagine, the usual stuff, so I sat down in an empty place next to one of the children and told them I am going to write today and they mustn't interrupt me for a few moments while I got my first draft down, and they were brilliant! They let me write.

Later, Beth reflected how this writing had 'made me feel better – I'd expressed myself, and now I had something, a tangible object, to look at, to help me reflect on my feelings. I suppose it enabled me to learn about my feelings, too.' Graves suggests that teachers compose publicly with their classes, writing on an overhead projector and talking about their writing as they write.

Children sometimes express in drawings (through the elements of design) and writing (through metaphor, simile, rhythm, alliteration, assonance, rhyme and other means) what they cannot easily talk about. And then the drawing and the writing may release them into talking about whatever is concerning, or even obsessing them. I have written before with my wife (Sedgwick and Sedgwick 1993) about how a girl who was being bullied first expressed her pain through a painting of her own face crossed out, and I have met bereaved children who have not talked about any aspect of their loss until they have written about it. The drawing and the writing enables the child to put enough distance between themselves and their experience for them to articulate their feelings.

A four-year-old boy who draws his head with large eyes and mouth, but no ears, turns out, when I meet him, to be profoundly deaf (see Sedgwick and Sedgwick 1993:64). These children, drawing their disabilities or their anger, offer us a glimpse into their emotions – and, as Mary Jane Drummond (1993:42) says,

> Without doing violence to our understanding of children as human beings, we cannot ignore either the emotional turbulence of their lives, or the emotional development that runs alongside the physical, social and cognitive changes that we see talking places in our schools and classrooms.

This chapter is about children beginning to write, and writing's relationship to drawing. In terms of their marks, children communicate through, first, drawings; second, drawings that are combined with (and in various ways similar to) writing; and third, writing itself. Humankind's early experiences communicating through visual images (cave pictures, hieroglyphics, pictograms) teach us to examine drawings and writing by children made before school in those homes, nurseries and play schools to find out about that 'emotional development' that is, all too often perhaps, 'turbulent'.

5

THE WRITING CORNER

In this chapter, I suggest that every classroom would benefit
from an area which the children know is dedicated to writing,
and I describe a classroom with such an area.

In Beth's classroom of five to seven year olds, as in many other good classrooms these days, there is a writing corner. There is also a science corner and
an art corner. Another day, she tells me, there'll be a technology corner, a
maths corner and an IT corner. Her classroom is like a little university, where
you go to a different area to study whatever matters to you. The fact that every
faculty, or department, isn't open every day is merely due to constraints of
time and space. But there's always a writing corner because (she tells me,
quoting the Bee Gees) 'words are all we have'. Her five year olds can get all
they need in this classroom to enable them to place writing at the centre of
their school experience; to help them know about its status as a means of
communication with themselves and with each other; to make it, at one and
the same time, both an everyday thing and an important thing.

On this writing table the children find: paper of different sizes, shapes and
colours; forms (while adults hate filling in forms, many children love it); little
pads for messages; an old Olivetti with a sheet of A4 already wound in; all
kinds of markers (pencils, crayons, ballpoints, felt-tips); office accessories,
such as a hole-punch, a pencil sharpener, sticky tape, rulers; old diaries. Many
writers enjoy the feel of the tools of their trade, and it becomes clear from
watching Beth's classroom for any length of time that child-writers do too.

And there is a post-box. One day I looked at the 'mail' that had been put
inside this box, and I found a curious document which when typed up (the
pencil is too faint to reproduce it in facsimile) looks like this:

PAAleLDb
APDDelALeDbel
DaooklAALeDbd
lLDESYDeSED

Danee
EEeilLD

This is clear evidence of a young child beginning to enjoy letters and understand what their purpose is. It is easy to underestimate this kind of communication, and, as a profession, we have underestimated it for years. That you and I cannot understand the writer's marks doesn't detract from their meaning any more than the intelligibility of early drafts or daubs make those drafts or daubs of no use to the poet or artist.

On some days, Beth has her class computer in this area as well, equipped with a word processing package and a printer. On the wall behind the writing corner is a display of the children's work. The items in the corner are changed from time to time. There are, for example, templates that look, before the children have used them, like this

I love you _____
even though _____

and some of the children have filled them in:

I love you Dad
even though fret [fart]

I love you Ayesha
even though you
snor

I love you Nana Betty
even though you
let Darrell into your room.

I love you Mum and Dad
even though you
don't let me sleep in your bed.

I love you Cordell
even though
you hit me every day

In using these simple templates, the child-writers hint at all sorts of domestic crises, and make attempts to come to terms with them. Thus the writing corner has a value that goes beyond learning about language. It helps children with life itself, not only with its celebrations and its disasters, but with its irritations too.

All these children can write. That is important. What is even more important is that they know they can. It is only basic respect on our part to acknowledge those two central facts about young children and the written word. The child who says to me (a visiting writer) 'I can't write' is not telling me anything about herself (though she may think she is), but about what someone has taught her. In Stalin County Primary the children have been trained to believe that writing = spelling. This is to imprison children. This cell is even more secure than the reading primer.

Here is another template:

I like/hate the feel/taste/touch of . . . because . . .

Two of the children have written:

I like the feel of bread because it is bumpy as a bouncy castle.

I like the feel of the onion because it is crumbly like a butterfly's wings when they've just come out of the chrysalis.

One day, Beth read her class my 'Poem about Love' (originally published in Sedgwick 1997b, but written for one of those anthologies I was criticising on p. 65):

Rebecca fancies Robert.
    Robert dreams of Dee.
Dee is crazy about Dave
    But Dave just wants his tea.

Mary Jane McMullen loves
    A boy who's in Year Eight –
He's asked Mary's sister
    Sally for a date

But Dave just wants his tea.

Larry's girl is Anne-Louise
    (Or so Larry has said)
But Anne-Louise kissed Lenny twice
    Behind the cricket shed

But Dave just wants his tea.

Farida dotes on Darren,
    Darren's darling's Jen.
Jen kissed Jonathan and Jack
    And James – and Jack again

But Dave just wants his tea

Anna's beau is Andrew.
    Andrew can't stand her
While Maggie, Meg and Margaret
    Only fancy Sir

But Dave just wants his tea.

Freda fancies Fariq,
    Fariq's girl is Gus.
The vicar says, surprisingly,
    God loves the lot of us

But Dave just wants his tea.

Later, pieces of paper appeared in the writing corner. The children have filled bubbles comic-wise saying 'I want Rebecca', 'I hate Rebecca', 'I love her', 'God loves the lot of us', 'Watch out, here comes a boy' and 'You shouldn't'. David can be seen in two pictures with bubbles with food in them, and the vicar is coming down with a parachute: a sky pilot?

The everyday aspect of writing that the writing corner serves better than anything else needs to be augmented frequently by oddness, by the unanticipated. Children need to be surprised and delighted into writing, as this seven year old was. He and his classmates had been asked to write something that had to be entirely composed of lies – and not just little fibs, but great big whoppers. He had written his piece on the writing table, the first part in pencil, the rest (when it became available) on the word processor:

Left Knee

My left knee has a pair of hands. It sometimes eats frogs. It has a mouth the size of a hippo. It plays a little game of frisbee with the stars when it is finished it goes for a swim with tissue paper in the toilet it plays snooker when people go to the toilet then

Snap

A girl had written her lies at the same time:

I love maths so much
that I dance with the numbers
and hula hoop with the circles
and I dance around the cross.

And another boy had written:

> I love writing so much
> I do it everyday
> but my pencil
> does all the spellings wrong
> it's got a magnet
> to wrong spellings.

Once on a course that I was running a young teacher told a group of teachers about the writing corner in her room. It sounded much like Beth's. But when she finished, a man said 'You can't have that sort of organisation now, because OFSTED want timetables for everything. That's more or less what we used to call an integrated day.' This seemed to me to be an interesting example of using modern developments in education management, especially in terms of accountability, to hoick classrooms back to bad old days, when children had no control over what they wanted to write, and when they wanted to write, and how they wanted to write it. In any event, the young teacher had the perfect answer: 'We had an OFSTED inspection last term,' she said quietly. 'And they loved my writing corner.'

Finally, an example of a nursery child writing in the sense of composing. That is to say, Ben is not putting pen to paper, or finger to keyboard, as he makes this poem.

> I go up the farm
> and walk the doggies up the track near the road.
> It has got stones and tiles like slabs.
> We see an old train and a new train.
> When there are no passengers the trains don't come.
> There are tractors and my Grandad's hedgecutter.
> It is noisy and it crashes into things.
> My Grandad nearly crashed into the fence
> and on to the track where we walk the dog.
> I have a cup of tea and then we go home.
> We go back and feed the dogs.

Here is the poem again with notes in square brackets suggesting what had provoked each line:

> I go up the farm [I admit, as the teacher, that I am responsible for the line endings] and walk the doggies up the track near the road. [I had asked about things that Ben did when he was enjoying himself]
> It has got stones and tiles like slabs. [Ben – tell me – What is the path like? . . . What are the tiles like?]

85

We see an old train and a new train. [What do you see when you go there?]

When there are no passengers the trains don't come. [This was unsolicited]

There are tractors and my Grandad's hedgecutter. [What else is there?]

It is noisy and it crashes into things. [What's that hedgecutter like?]

My Grandad nearly crashed into the fence [Like what?]

and on to the track where we walk the dog.

I have a cup of tea and then we go home. [What happens next?]

We go back and feed the dogs.

Politicians concerned about children and writing often forget that professional writers use tools other than pen and paper, or word processors, to compose. They dictate. And nursery writers are particularly amenable to this technique, which is here not just about writing, but also about teaching. I sat at a computer, asked the children questions, and simply wrote their answers down, paying as much attention as I possibly could under the circumstances of a noisy nursery; and then basing my next questions on their replies. This section could have appeared anywhere in this book; especially in the reading section, because Ben read words he had composed off the screen. 'I go to the – ' I read, pointing to the last word. And Ben confidently shouted 'farm'. This happened several times as I read to him.

6

DEAR JERLISA,
DEAR LEISHA . . .

Chapter 6 is largely dedicated to a correspondence between six
six-year-old children and myself, and an analysis of some of the
issues the correspondence raised.

Developing writing in the classroom

Can children under the age of six write? To every educational question (as to
every other kind), there is a simple answer that is wrong. Here is today's:

Of course, some have always been able to write and always will, and
most haven't.

This is the answer accepted by most adults. It seems to express an implicit
belief in a moment when a child changes from being a non-writer to being a
writer. It is as though we might see a child change from being a non-crawler
to a crawler in one dramatic moment, or from being a non-talker to being a
fluent conversationalist, able to discuss the news, perhaps, and the relative
qualities of the latest bands, and the prices of chicken nuggets in one
sentence. It makes more sense to me to see the child as a potential writer from
the beginning, and to see the earliest scribbles as proto-writing. The child
needs, in the infant class, to be encouraged to believe in him or herself as
(among many other things) a writer. I watched a classroom at work (Beth's
again) where this belief is implicit in everything done in it, and I print below
my notes:

Twenty-nine six-year-olds are sitting on the carpet in the classroom.
The first thing I noticed about the classroom is a writing corner.
The children in this classroom, then, are treated as writers treat
themselves. I can't imagine how much I'd swear if, every time I
was uncertain about the spelling of a word, I wasn't free to write it
down until I'd had the spelling checked by someone older and bigger

than me, or looking it up in a dictionary, or carting around a word book . . .

The rest of the room is typical of a lively modern infant classroom. The children are studying 'Ourselves', and there are baby photographs of everyone, including the teacher, on the wall. Elsewhere there is a display of working models, made by the children, with a notice that says 'PLEASE TOUCH'. Several of the models look the worst for wear, in the way that a well-read book looks: decrepit, friendly, used. The classroom arrangement means the children face each other rather than the blackboard.

There are books everywhere, not class sets of reading books, but new picture books, and poetry books, and information books and poetry books. There is a little library of books that the children have made themselves. The children's drawings and paintings are displayed everywhere, in the Plowden style.

What is there none of? No housepoint boards. No star sheets, with Rachael and James ahead of the pack, and Darren and Sharon at the back with only two stars each. There are few commercially-produced products – posters and the like – and, where there are such things, they are mixed with the children's images. There are no notices suggesting different ways of beginning a story: ONCE UPON A TIME. ONCE THERE WAS . . .

The teacher says 'I want you to think about a time when you were very angry . . . What was it that made you angry?' The responses concern domestic arguments with parents and brothers and sisters, mostly: 'I get angry when my mummy says you can't watch television; when my sister messes up my bedroom; when the cat scratches me.' 'Once I was eating my dinner and my sister said look there and she pushed my face in my dinner.' But one child talks about a fight she had with another girl on the playground the day before. 'Me and Melanie stopped being friends yesterday . . . I scratched her and she scratched me . . .' As she talks about it the two girls smile sheepishly at each other.

Then the teacher asks the class a series of questions:

What colour are you deep inside [she presses her heart] when you're very angry?
What shapes are you inside when you are very angry?
Can you show us all what your faces look like when they are angry?
What do you feel like inside?

Red and purple triangles abound in answer to the first two questions. Many of the faces show what I would call cartoon anger – breath held, puce coloured skin, gritted teeth – but three of the children convey a more realistic impression. Mouths are thinned to a line and a wide stare is in the eyes. A cold, sulky, brooding anger seems to me to be more authentic than the rage suggested by the puce skin, the gritted teeth of the cartoon. Children say vivid sentences in answer to the last question: 'I feel like a bomb that is going to explode . . . I feel hot – ' ('Hot as what?' the teacher asks. There is a longish pause. The child looks uncomfortable for a moment, and then says, 'Hot like a fire', and is extravagantly praised for this conventional simile).

The teacher gets the other children to look at the three authentic faces. 'Look at her eyes . . . his teeth . . . his lips . . . ' Now I want you to go away and draw your faces when they are angry . . . You might have a look in the mirror before you start, and show yourself your angry face. I want the drawing just to be your face, but you might put your angry hands in it as well . . . ' Here the children show each other their fists: whitened knuckles, fingernails jammed into their palms.

There is a choice of paper available for the children: Charlotte's and Robert's are on A4, Holly's on A3. While the children are drawing, the teacher goes around praising and encouraging. Eventually, I notice that she is talking to each child about words:

'What are you saying as your face looks like this? Perhaps you could put a bubble coming out of the mouth telling us? . . . What's going on here? Write a line about it . . . ' To a child who is clearly already fluent with writing, she says, 'Can you write a sentence telling us how you felt when that was happening?' The children don't need to be told that it doesn't matter about the spelling, because that is a vital part of the culture of the classroom, and has been since September when class and teacher met, and indeed was part of the culture in their classes before that, as well.

Soon most of the children had written on their work, and a session begins that I now see is a very important part of the process. The children, after play, sit again on the carpet, and the teacher takes each drawing/writing in turn and talks to us about what the artist/ writer is telling us. She makes a point of referring to both the drawings and the words, and in every case, she suggests some way the communication might go forward.

I reproduce some of the drawings in Chapter 3. In Charlotte's writing, it is interesting to note how she ends as she began, with the phrase about the beach. She knows this rounds the story off neatly, without, probably, ever being told so:

I hated it when my nan and Grandad too me to the beach I did not like it I through a paddie I went red on my face and I went near the rowing boat and I felt sad I didn't want to go to the beach

Holly's writing says

> I feel like a sucau [circle] and I went rilly red so so so so so so red I am
> so angry I feel I word [would] leave the house and say bubey [bye bye]
> rode [rude] very very rude . . . You idett I hate you. You are so stupid

Other vivid sentences from this session that are redolent of children's
domestic problems were 'My sister make me mad be cause she wis [winds] me
up . . . my mum didot [didn't] let me go eway [away] wan [when] I
dut [didn't] little [like] my tey . . . .' And some referred to the classroom:
'I felt mad with miss Tinning be cause miss Tinning said I had to do PE
when I felt sick.'

By contrast to this school, another teacher says, 'Oh, but they're only five,
they can't write.' Or in the same school, there is a class of six and seven year
olds. These children can write, or most of them can. But they are not allowed
to until the spelling of each word has been checked by the teacher (or one of
those other people – though it has to be said that their presence is less likely
in schools like this).

The Raeburn Letters

My title for this section suggests a chest uncovered in some old house packed
with quill-penned parchment, on which I could read with some help the
details of a family's history. In fact, Raeburn is an infant school on an estate in
Ipswich. The visitor is struck on entering the school (once he or she has
managed to break through the security system) by the teachers' confidence in
the children and the children's friendliness and enthusiasm.

I had, for a long time, been impressed by Robinson *et al.*'s work in *Some Day
You Will No All About Me* (1990). This book, named with a quotation from a
child, is a series of letters between an American academic and a group of
young children in a school in England. I decided to write to a group of
children in my wife's class of six year olds at Raeburn to see what development
in the children's writing I would notice over a school year. More importantly,
I wanted to see how the children would build a relationship with me largely
through the written word. The notion of corresponding with someone with
a serious purpose – to find out about them and their lives, and to tell them
about our own lives – was potentially a far richer experience than many language experiences children have these days because of the insistent demands
of the National Curriculum. Also, narrowing pronouncements by ignorant
ministers about literacy hours, and cutting back on geography, history and
art to make way for 'an hour a day more literacy' – as though children didn't
use words in other subjects – mean that language events in context, as these
letters would be, were becoming more and more important as each month and
each lunacy from the government went by.

I wrote:

14 November

CAN YOU HELP ME?

I've heard you like writing. Would you be my penfriend? I am the husband of Mrs Sedgwick.

Would you write a letter every now and then for a while? If so, give your letter to Mrs Sedgwick. Say yes, and tell me something about yourself.

It doesn't have to be spelt right!

I will reply to your letters.

Some of them will come out in a book I am writing. That's why I need your help.

Yours, with best wishes
Fred

The children already knew me a little, because I had visited the school frequently and read and recited poems and stories to them. They knew I was a writer – mainly through my poems for children. Dawn told me they were very keen to participate in this experiment. Eventually she chose six children. During the year, some of the other children were not above pretending they were in the group: that was the value the children placed on the project.

I decided not to avoid my correspondents while I was writing to them. Admittedly, if I had, this would have produced a more rigorous exploration of part of my hypothesis: that children could use letters received and sent to build a relationship with a stranger. But I felt it was unnatural not to visit a school, or at least a classroom, I had come to know well over the previous year. I braved the new post-Dunblane security system to see the children whenever I felt like it and whenever it was convenient for Dawn.

Jerlisa wrote her first letter (Illustrations 13 and 14):

18th November
Dear Fred
I am Jerlisa
I am 5
I liek simmg
in my pool
Is November

from Jerlisa

Throughout the children's letters, I have, mostly, tried to preserve the look of them either by printing them in facsimile or by recording children's errors in my transcription with, where necessary, explanatory corrections in square

Illustration 13: Jerlisa

brackets. Here, though, I don't believe 'simmg', given the 'pool' in the next line, needs explaining. It is, indeed, an example of how children in good schools today are prepared to attack words they can't spell correctly. To think I was told when I was young that if I couldn't spell a word I should think of a simpler synonym! This did nothing for my prose style in my early adolescent years, as I routinely wrote 'needed' for 'necessary', 'pulled apart' for 'separated' and 'very, very worried' for 'desperate'. Dawn tells the children that, as long as

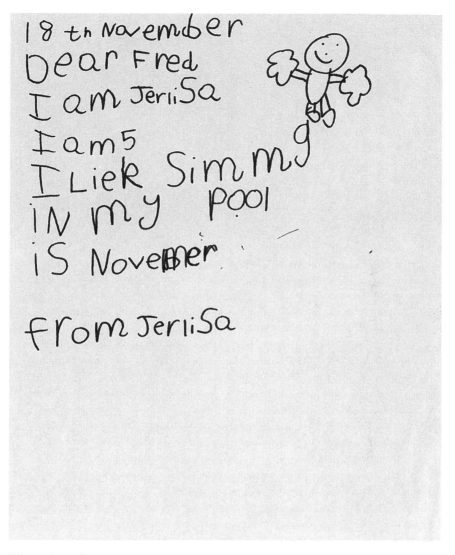

Illustration 14

they can read the word themselves, that is good enough. There is a huge political issue here that can be expressed thus: children who must, by the rules of the classroom, check the spelling of every word with an adult before they are allowed to use it in writing, are under a rigid control. I will explore this later in Chapter 8.

Leisha's first letter (Illustration 15) is more difficult to read than Jerlisa's and I rely here on the classroom assistant's transcription:

Illustration 15

by Leisha 18th November
Dear Fred
My home is
I am Leisha
I am 5

94

I like my cat
I like my car
I like to go to the zoo
I like to play in the paddling pool on Saturday
from Leisha

This letter (typically I was to learn) is decorated with drawings of a heart and a little girl. I have argued in chapter 4 that drawings are more important in the context of children's writing than we have conventionally believed. Here, Leisha's heart, and her little girl, are little less than offerings of friendship. It is worth comparing the appearances of the two letters because I think they are indicative of two different characters: Leisha, spontaneous, hit-and-miss much of the time; Jerlisa precise, neat, orderly. Obviously, a more old-fashioned way of describing this difference would be to say Leisha is 'untidy' or 'scrappy'; to feel that the junior teachers will need to work hard to bring her presentation up to scratch, while Jerlisa has already learned much about the importance of neatness.

Kieran's first letter also says 'I am Leisha'. One of the oldest problems emerged right at the beginning: he was obviously copying the girl next to him! Once again, there are two ways of looking at this. Traditionally, he was cheating, and the junior teachers might well have to separate him from Leisha if this habit persists. On the other hand, he sees himself as being in difficulties, and finds one way out of them. He is not a cheat at all: he is a resourceful writer in the early stages of the craft. He also told me that he liked climbing trees; though, as with all Kieran's early letters, I wouldn't have known this without the transcription that Elaine, the classroom assistant, had provided.

Shaun wrote after the date (about which they were always very conscientious) 'my name is Shaun Saturday is my beadae [birthday] I am goyne [going] to dee [be] 6'. As with Jerlisa's letter, that 'beadae' is heartening in that it is an attempt at a word that is not entirely open to a child's phonetic analysis. While in the late 1970s, we would have seen it as merely an error, we can see it now as a staging post on the road to literacy.

Isaac's letter said:

18th November
Dear Fred
I am 5
I am Isaac
I like simmg [swimming]
fomr Isaac

Obviously, the swimming was a subject that my correspondents had shared as they began the difficult and strange task of opening their part of a correspondence. Sharna told me, among other things, that she liked *The Village in the Snow* (a reading book).

It struck me when reading these first letters that children are very open about themselves, and therefore vulnerable. There are ethical issues here: should Dawn and I have discussed the project with the parents first? We hadn't, and at least one of the parents showed some anxiety about the relationship. Even more important, there is an ethical issue in children's writing in general. I am not going to explore it here, except to ask some questions. Should children have notebooks in school that are private? How careful are we about publishing – in assembly, on the walls, in school newspapers – what children write? Do we allow children to keep silent about what they written if they feel they need to? How would a professional writer feel if we peered over his or her shoulder, and made a sentence or paragraph or page 'better'?

I replied quickly to these letters. It was important to show that my overture to the children had been sincere. All of us who like receiving letters have known what disappointment is, and have caused disappointment. A letter may be unanswered, a phone call unreturned, because of our friend's or colleague's pressure of work, but it always feels, for some little time at least, like a slight. And to slight writers beginning their first correspondence would be unforgivable and, of course, might have a serious effect on their attitudes to letters in the future.

I had very little idea what the exercise would produce. I hoped that I would see significant development in the children's grasp of written language and also, through the children setting more and more of their own agenda, a bridge growing between us. This was a classic example of learning as I went along as I wrote my letters and read the children's; as I wrote this commentary, I was living with uncertainty, and it wasn't always comfortable. The neatness in print of this account belies the reality of my experience. Looking at what I wrote in the letters now, I suppose I was trying to open the children's letters out by asking questions, always, if I could, picking up something the writer had told me in his or her letter.

21 November 1996

Dear Jerlisa

Thank you for your lovely letter. I am glad you like swimming in your pool. I am not very good at swimming. How do you think I might get better at it?

It also seemed important to try and say something about myself, hence my admission about my poor (in fact more or less non-existent) swimming. I think this was connected to my perception that the children had been frank, and therefore I should be too.

Dear Kieran

I loved your letter. Be careful climbing those trees. Have you ever fallen out of a tree?

Dear Isaac

Thank you for your terrific letter with the drawing. Where do you go swimming?

The children had, of course, already set a significant part of the agenda – the swimming.

Dear Sharna

What a great letter you sent me! Have you got a cat and a dog? What is the story in The Village in the Snow about?

Dear Leisha

Thank you for your terrific letter. What are your favourite animals at the zoo? I like tortoises because they are slow and have lovely patterns on their shells.

Dear Shaun

I loved your letter. How did the party go? Did you have a good time? What games did you play?

The replies were dated 25 November. Jerlisa's said:

Dear Fred
I am 5
Thank you for your.
lovely letter. I am.
swimming in my.
pool I will get yow.
better at it.
form Jerlisa

I think this is a fine letter. In her characteristically firm, neat handwriting, Jerlisa has had the wit to copy one of my sentences in her reply, assuming this would be correct in spelling and grammar ('Thank you for your lovely letter'.) Second, she has made a generous offer to coach me in my swimming! Once more we see that candid vulnerability that will last only another six or seven years. And look at the full stops. Jerlisa knows about them, and roughly what they are for. The fact that they are not in the right places should not make us worry. Instead we should be pleased that the writer has grasped some of their significance – partly from her general reading, partly from her reading scheme, and partly, I hope, from my letters.

Leisha's letter (Illustration 16) is, once again, all over the place: three rectangles contain drawings of animals: a tortoise, a cat, and some other creature, probably from the zoo that she likes. These illustrations show that Leisha has learnt from books that drawings work together with words to convey information and impressions. She recycles information she has already given me (it is safe to begin a letter 'I am 5'), but nevertheless picks up my expressed liking for tortoises. Sharna ignores my questions, and tells me that her cat is called 'Sarnam'. Shaun, however, tells me about his party: 'my party good/ it wet good'. Isaac tells me that he 'go to Crpol [Crown Pools]', and Kieran assures me that he has not fallen out of a tree; though, again, I would have found his letter completely illegible if it weren't for Elaine's transcription on the back.

I replied:

29 November 1996

Dear Jerlisa

Thank you for writing again. It was kind of you to say you would make me better at swimming, but that would be difficult.

I like books and stories. Have you got a story you could tell me? Your favourite one?

This is a crude attempt at provoking a longer letter, as was the next one:

Dear Leisha

Thank you for your letter. I like pigs, too. I once carried a piglet into my Grandma's house, and she smacked me. Have you ever done anything naughty like that?

ps I loved the drawings

Leisha always had, throughout the correspondence, drawings on her letters. I wanted to encourage this, and to see if my encouragement would pass to the others.

Dear Sharna

Thanks for your letter. Sirnaya [this is how the name had been transcribed by Elaine] is an interesting name for a cat. My cat is called Stanley. He chews the carpet. What does your cat do?

25th November

Dear Fred

I am 5
I like reosinThePool
My Name is Leisha
I Like pyinthezoo.
IPo
I Like pywl From I ho
1996 go
Leisha ca
brown cat
Fran
Leisda

Illustration 16

Dear Shaun

I am sorry to hear you weren't well. Are you better now? I have a bad
knee sometimes. It's all right at the moment.

Dear Isaac

Thank you for your letter. Crown Pools is noisy, isn't it?
    Do you swim in the sea, too?

Dear Kieran

Thank you for your letter. My son fell out of a tree and hurt himself
quite badly, but he was all right quite soon afterwards. We must take
care of ourselves!
    What else do you do?

How did the children respond to these attempts? Jerlisa simply told me a
story (Illustration 17):

Ten December 1996
Dear Fred
Floppy brrri [barked] at a cat
The cat rbby [runned] up a tree
Bilff was cioss wiff Foppy
and Bilff was up a tree
Bilff was in a pool
Foppy was in a cat tree
Foppy was in a pool
Bilff was in a pool
                    from Jerlisa

Jerlisa uses in this letter not only names from a reading scheme but its
repetitive rhythms, its flat tone and its dreary plot. Even the most banal
literature has an effect on children's writing. What would happen if children
were allowed to encounter the first-rate from the beginnings of their experiences with books? David McKee instead of Floppy and Biff? Any number of
brilliant writer-illustrators for children instead of the Village with Three
Corners? There are at least two contrasted ways of seeing children as human
beings that are relevant here: are they passive acquirers of certain basic skills,
or active, imaginative inheritors of a tradition, which they interpret with the
knowledge those clouds of glory have generously given them?

    Shaun ignores my knee, but Isaac and Sharna both pick up information
I had passed to them. Isaac tells me that, yes 'I do go en the cey [sea] Fred',
and Sharna responds to my enquiry by saying 'My cat scratched me'. Kieran
simply tells me that he loved my letter.

    I visited the children in school at this point. I recited and read to the whole
class poems by Charles Causley (1996) and myself, as well as some playground
rhymes. I then showed my six correspondents a simple structure for making a

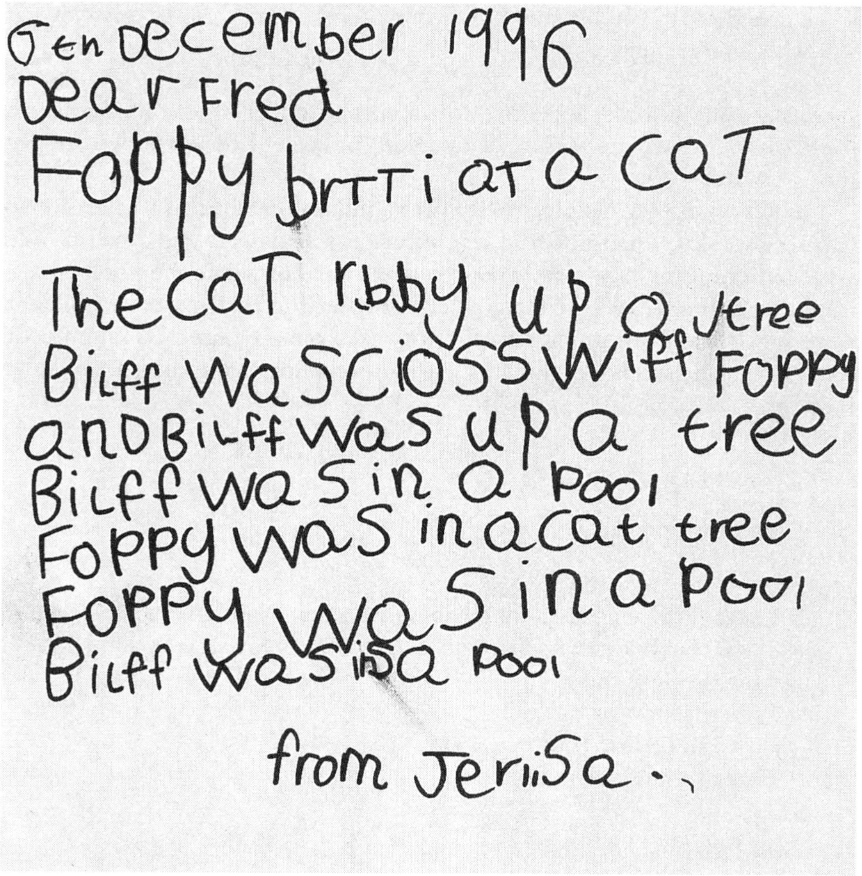

Illustration 17

poem. I suggested they made sentences on halved A4 paper along the lines of 'I used to . . . but now I . . .'.

Also, just before Christmas, I met Jerlisa at church, where she was taking part in a multi-faith service. I then received some communications that were not provoked by letters from me. Leisha, for example, gave two envelopes made by her stapling sheets of paper in half, and inside her makeshift envelopes she wrote, 'To Fred I am 5 yeold I like goin the poan from Leisha'. Anyone who visits schools with young children will be familiar with these scraps of paper, handed over towards the end of the day. 'I did this picture for you'; 'This is a poem I wrote'. No documents in schools have more variant meaning between the giver and the receiver. Mostly adults throw them away as soon as they are clear of the school. I asked a child what these gifts meant:

I give them to you because I like your poems . . . I'm gonna miss you
when you're gone.

A teacher said: 'I think these little documents are offers of, or confirmations of
friendship . . . They are saying, "I like you" or even "I hope you will respect
me as a writer".'

I did not write my next letters for over a month. Partly, this was because of
Christmas. Also, I had not read the letters as a sequence, and I had no idea
what I might learn; how rich or poor the data were, or where the whole project
might be going. I was discouraged: even my feeling that my correspondents
were keenly awaiting my letters did not make me act faster. Picking up the
letters after Christmas was difficult without worrying along the lines of What
is it for?

7 January 1997

Dear Shaun

Happy New Year to you!
    I haven't written for a long time. I am sorry. You wrote to me last
on your birthday, 6th December last year. How have you been
getting on since then?
    I loved your writing:
    I used to be little but now I am big.
    Please write soon.

Dear Jerlisa

In your last letter you told me all about Biff and Floppy. It was
brilliant.
    Did you enjoy the service at the church? I thought you were very
brave. Tell me how you felt in your next letter, please.
    Happy New Year to you!
    Please write soon.

Dear Isaac

Your last letter was about going in the sea. It was brilliant. What
have you been doing since then?
    Happy New Year to you!
    Please write to me soon.

Dear Sharna

Your last letter was ages ago, and I haven't written. Sorry. It was about your cat scratching you. I hope your cat has been good since.

Happy New Year to you!

How is school going? Please write soon, as I enjoy reading your letters.

Dear Kieran

I am glad you liked my letter. I liked yours, too.

What did you do in the holidays? I hope you had a good time. I went to a football match and Father Christmas brought me lots of books.

Happy New Year to you!

Please write again.

Dear Leisha

I loved your letter, with its envelope made with staples. Thank you.

I loved the drawing, too.

Could you write a letter to me about things you like doing – with drawings and words in it?

Happy New Year to you!

Please write soon.

The replies came. Under a smiley face, Jerlisa referred to my question about the church:

I love the church
Its the next church
I do no [know] the church

The full stops, right or wrong, had gone. Leisha told me that she had got 'Barbie and Ken' for Christmas, and added not only her address, but also her postcode. Once again, she told me that she was five, adding 'I live at 97 F_____ Road'. Sharna assured me that her cat wouldn't scratch her anymore. Shaun characteristically ignored my letter's contents, but he gave another sentence for the 'I used to . . . ' poem: 'I used to play with my railway now I do not love from Shaun.'

I wrote again about various matters, but I feel that the reader has experienced enough of my words in this correspondence, and so do not reproduce them here.

I received replies on 27 January. Shaun, for once, directly referred to my letter, telling me that he liked playing cards. Kieran relied on an old standby

Illustration 18

of many a recipient of letters (I had done this several times during this correspondence): 'I loved your letter'. Isaac assured me that he 'bib get the bike for Christmas'. Sharna's cat had scratched her again. Jerlisa told me that she had to go to the hairdresser's and have her hair 'platd', but I don't know what 'I no you/I no I no' refers to here.

Leisha's letter (Illustration 18) stood out. This is how Elaine had transcribed it from the child's dictation:

27 January 1997

Dear Fred

I was angry because my Grandad died. I am happy I am sad I am playing with Victoria.

Love Leisha

For the first time, a universal issue, death, had emerged in the letters. There was such honesty about this letter ('angry'), and the writer's confusion was expressed in 'I am happy I am sad I am playing', and in the even more frenetic presentation. I am always impressed when something serious and huge and overwhelming imposes itself on my work as a teacher. 'Where's the Grandad/ who told me stories/when I was four?/In Heaven' a child wrote in response to a poem I describe in Sedgwick (1997a). Here I think we can say that the relationship between myself and Leisha has developed during the correspondence. Her vulnerability has become a frankness, and the letters have given her the opportunity to write something that will help her reflect on a bereavement.

On 22 February 1997 I wrote about playing cards (Shaun), the spring and the weather (everyone) the bike Isaac got for Christmas, Sharna's cat and Jerlisa's hair. I also wrote to Leisha: 'You told me in your letter about your Grandad. I am very sorry that he died.'

In her reply, Sharna carried on with her cat data. She confirmed the scratch incident, but told me that it also 'climbs tree and purrs'. Kieran will 'pla outsid' in the spring. Leisha's letters are often more complicated than the others:

I play was[with] Sarah + Victoria we play Mairy Popopn we play unbrellas from Leisha

I was disappointed that she didn't tell me more about her Grandad. Shaun is also looking forward to the spring, while Jerlisa wrote (Illustration 19).

Illustration 19

Dear Fred
24th February
I love my hair plaited
it is lovely to have
my hair plaited
her[e] is a piccr
of my[me]
love from Jerlisa

On 27 February 1997, very quickly for me, I replied with more effort, so I reproduce all my letters for that date. They contained a sentence in common – 'I enjoy your letters – I have just read them all again' – because I wanted to suggest to the children how important the correspondence was to me. Also, these letters all contained dreadful drawings.

Dear Jerlisa

Thank you for your picture of you with your hair plaited and in your pink dress.

Tell me something exciting that happened to you. You could write about it, and draw it.

I once went to Egypt, and Mrs Sedgwick got on a camel! She was frightened.

I laughed. Our son Daniel laughed.

Dear Shaun

I hope you enjoy playing with your brother in the spring.

Tell me something funny that once happened to you. I once got stuck on an icy road, and could not move, or I would have fallen over!

You could draw and write the funny thing.

Dear Isaac

They are terrific.

Don't go too fast on the bike!

When I was seven I fell off my scooter, so I have a broken front tooth. I will show it to you when I see you, if you ask me.

Dear Leisha

How do you play umbrellas? You could do a picture of you playing umbrellas. That might help me understand.

Dear Kieran

Tell me about some games you will play outside. Will you play 'It'?
    What about a picture of you playing outside?

Dear Sharna

Our cat killed a blackbird last night. Mrs Sedgwick saw it this
morning at the bottom of the stairs.
    I would love a picture of you and your cat.
    I am glad I didn't see the bird. I was still asleep.

My drawings were as follows: Jerlisa's letter showed 'Mrs Sedgwick on the
camel' with a bubble saying 'Oh dear!' Isaac had a drawing of my broken
tooth, labelled. Leisha's had a picture of a sad man under an umbrella,
labelled. Kieran had to make do with a picture of me saying 'Hello Kieran!'
Sharna had a picture of 'me asleep', with pillow and snore labelled. And Shaun
had a drawing of me on an icy road crying 'Help!!!' I hoped that these
multimedia communications might encourage the children to use different
ways of expressing their meanings.
    Here are their replies, which I received on 3 March:

Jerlisa S
65 —— Road
Ipswich
Suffolk
Dear Fred
My Brthiae Cordell
play'd weve Darrell
And My My brthiae
love us
Cordell Love My [me] and Darrell
from Jerlisa

Shaun also put his address at the top, then told me: 'I went on the fireman's
pole. Then I jumped down it.' Kieran wrote: 'I play outside with my brother.
We play Sticky toffee.' Sharna's letters told me: 'My cat stopped scratching
me. I went to the shops'; Isaac: 'My baby sister plays with my bricks' and,
finally, Leisha:

It is nearly my birthday
I am get for my birthday
a little stero
This is how

uoy play umbrella
love
from
Leisha

The attempt to provoke specific content was only partially successful.

There now followed another long break. This was partly due to the Easter holiday, and partly due to pressure of other work. I didn't reply to the children until 10 April, the first day of the summer term. I decided there was little point in picking up the issues in earlier letters, as they would have forgotten about them. I simply wrote the same letter to all of them, to see how they would respond:

10 April 1997

What a long time it is since I last wrote! Sorry.

What's been happening to you? I've been in the car a lot, driving hundreds of miles to work.

I am very pleased to see the warm spring weather. What do you do these days when you get home from school? Last night I went to Nacton shore with Mrs Sedgwick for a walk.

Do write soon with your drawings and sentences. I love to get them.

With love from
Fred

Jerlisa's writing had developed greatly over the five months: (Illustration 20).

15th April
Dear Fred
Weni I go home I play wive Cotney [Courtney]. Cotney plays a lot wive me. I like Cotney playeg wive me. I play wive Cotney evriy day Cotney com ronde miy hous. I play on my Nintendo. Wei did you go in your car
from Jerlisa

In Leisha's letter, the Spice Girls emerged for the first time in writing with children, showing the effect of a powerful media on even the youngest children:

Dear Fred We go home I play rond my [round mine – Suffolk for round my house] Victora was Sarah and play Spice gils I am Victora and is Sarah Emma Victora is Geri We ? spice girls love from Leisha

109

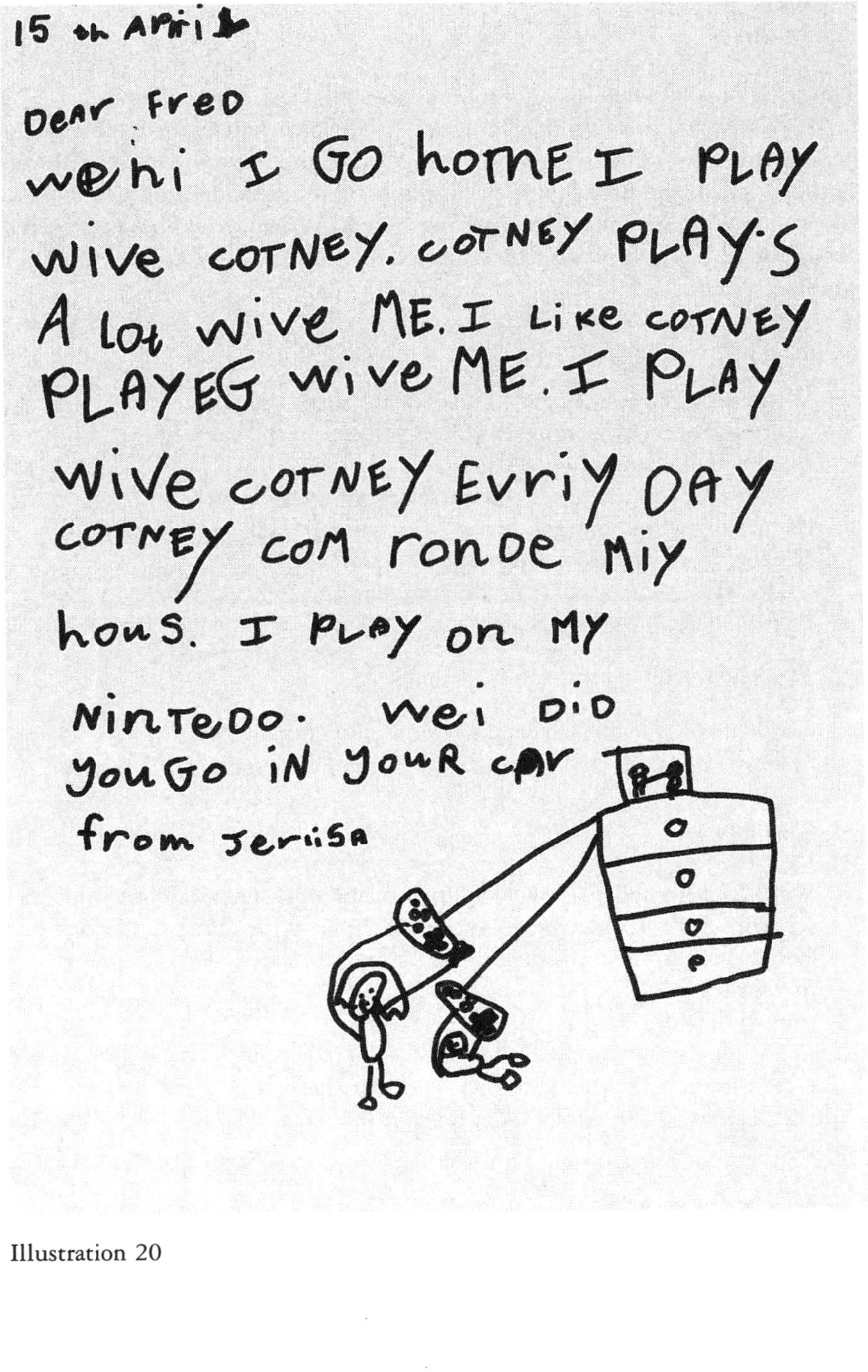

15 th April

Dear FreD
wehi I GO homE I PLAY
wive COTNEY. COTNEY PLAY's
A lot wive ME. I LiKE COTNEY
PLAYEG wive ME. I PLAY
wive COTNEY EvriY DAY
COTNEY COM ronDE MiY
houS. I PLAY on MY
NinTeDo. wei DiD
youGo iN youR cAr
from Jeriisa

Illustration 20

One point that Leisha's letters always raise is the relationship between content and presentation. Essays at secondary school, at college, and even on a theology course I am studying at the moment, are assessed as though these two components are unrelated to each other: there are marks out of ten for what the piece says, and marks out of ten for what it looks like. This flies in the face of reality, and all Leisha's letters make this, among other things, clear: her content is conveyed in large part through her presentation. The same is true of all the children's writing (and of all writing), but Leisha is the one whose work makes this point most obvious.

I have lost the other letters. Shameful, yes, but it happens with letters. My letters for 15 May 1997:

Dear Jerlisa

It is a month since you wrote. I hope you are well, and still friends with Courtney. You asked me, where did I go in my car? I have been to lots of places, like Durham and Slough and Stevenage.
Can you find them on a map?
Tell me what you have been doing.

Dear Isaac

Thank you for your letter. How are you?
Are you enjoying school? Is Mrs Sedgwick being good?
Please let me know when you can.

Dear Leisha

So you play Spice Girls. What do like about the Spice Girls? Who is your favourite? Why? I have never seen them sing. What are they like?

Dear Keiran

You play upstairs with your toys. What a good letter. What do you like doing best in school? I like writing best.

Dear Sharna

Is Emma still your friend? What do you do in school? How about doing a drawing of you in school doing something?

Dear Shaun

I hope you are well. I loved your last letter, a month ago. Tell all about what you do now the weather is warmer.

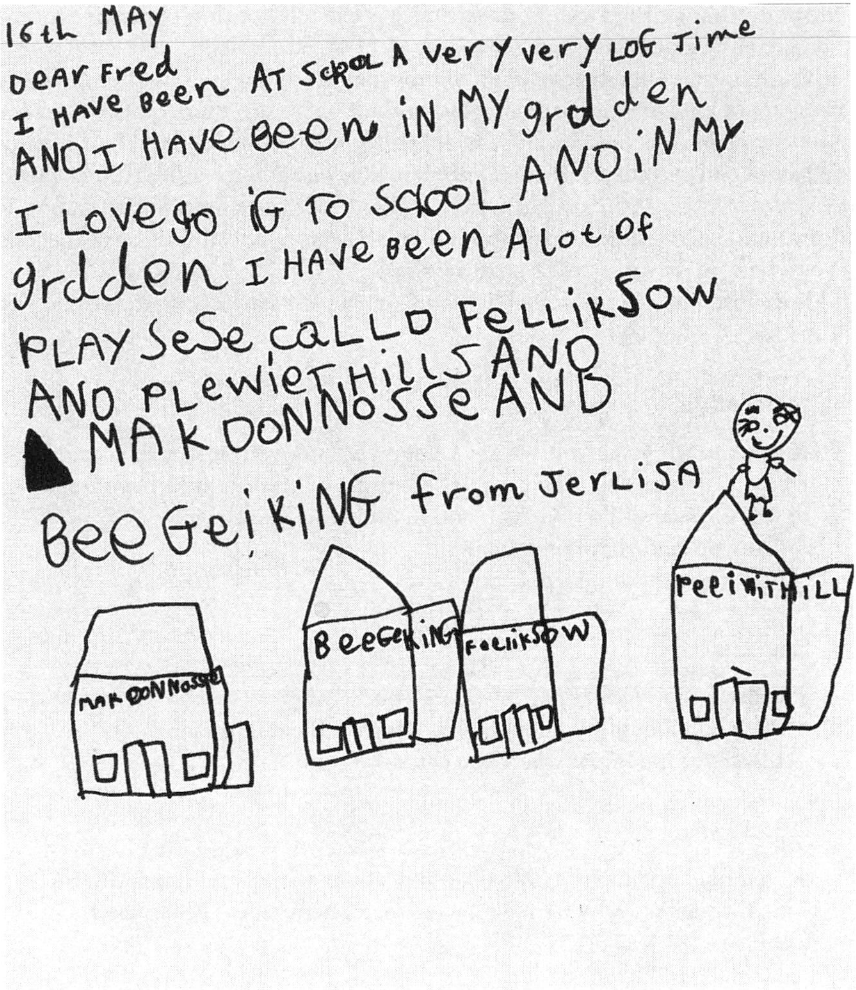

Illustration 21

In her fluent reply the next day (Illustration 21), Jerlisa picks up my questions:

> 16th May
> Dear Fred
> I have been at school a very very log [long] time
> and I have been in my grdden
> I love goig to school and in my
> grdden I have been a lot of
> playsese [places] calld Felliksow [Felixstowe]

and Plewiet hills [Pleasurewood Hills] and
Makdonnosse [McDonald's] and
Beegeiking [Burger King] from Jerlisa

As the correspondence drew towards a close, I began to focus more on Jerlisa and Leisha for the purposes of an interim article on children writing letters (Sedgwick 1997c). Leisha's letter on 16 May was typically free and easy, with drawings and her usual signs of warmth:

Dear Fred
I like you Fred
The red teddy
went to a hose [house]
I like Mrs Sedgwick
It [this] is what
the spice girls
look like
emma is
my fledsed [favourite]
spice girl
love from
Leisha

The last letters came on 18 July. Here is Jerlisa's

If you want to no wich class Im goin in Mr Hamsptens class . . . where are you going on the summer holidays? If you are going enny-where have a great time . . . I want to go to Dinyland Paresse I am going to Ameriker frest [first] entlen [?then] Lindr will take me to Disnyland Pareese I will go there on a plane I will meet Lindr at her house my cresins [?cousins] coming to ther names are Kelly Jade Jamie Darrell Leisha and Nana Betty Debby Tommy Traysy Jerelle . . .
    I like all your letters I wonder where you will go in September
Love from Jerlisa

Issac simply wrote: Dear Fred I am gonto [going to] Leeds and I am not cemen [coming] bec [back] I liek it in Lees . . . from Isaac.
    The way the Spice Girls pop up from time to time in that correspondence makes me reflect on how temporary their fame and influence will be (as I write) or has been (as you read) compared with the vigour and feeling the children use and show in their letters. I think the letters speak largely for themselves. Suffice it to say here that the children show evidence of development in terms of their relationship with me, and in terms of their

written language. The Raeburn letters are evidence, I believe, of the power of learning activities when the children are allowed to set the agenda; when they are not corrected all the time; and when there is an interest that is not only a school one. They also demonstrate the power of a context that is more than simply an hour in the day fixed by a secretary of state.

7

CHILDREN WRITING LISTS

In this chapter, following Myra Barrs (1987), I show how important a genre for children writing the list can be. The chapter ends with some older children exploring memories and emotions through the compiling of lists.

Barrs (1987) notes that 'two of the commonest genres' of writing used by children when not under teacher control are letters and lists. Although the letters quoted in Chapter 6 were, in fact, initiated by the teacher, I think they demonstrate the power of this genre to engage children. Barrs goes on to note that children are not good writers of non-narrative prose. I asked a seven year old to write 'something about cars' and I received after a few moments:

Cars are all sorts of colours. They go along the road. They take you to school. Mummys and daddys drive them.

And Barrs' point was demonstrated. But she says that children write lists of considerable vigour:

Chairs big ones little ones
Eating food
Mum talking to people
palying with friends
Eating backfast
raeding naespaper

This isn't surprising, as Barrs (1987) says

Many societies – perhaps most – have at some stage used lists to preserve their knowledge of the world. It is understandable that children, as they begin to map the world around them, should make use of lists to order what they know.

Indeed, many adults say that, when they are under stress because of the number of tasks waiting for them in a particular day, lists are a way of making them feel better. There is one such list on my desk in front of me at the moment:

> wab 1 and 2 (the computer file names for this book)
> psalm
> get books from library
> phone Essex school
> write HC
> poems for Cookson and Moses
> phone Falmer about Assembly Man
> collect pamphlets
> get something for lunch
> phone dentist & ITFC

Many poems are lists, like George Herbert's 'Prayer':

> Prayer the Churches banquet, Angels age,
>   Gods breath in man returning to his birth,
>   The soul in paraphrase, heart in pilgrimage,
> The Christian plummet sounding heav'n and earth;

A six year old dictates to his teacher:

> **Listen**
>
> I can hear patterns talking
> I can hear the clock chattering
> I can hear the egg timer whispering
> I can hear the calculator making numbers
> I can hear the chair walking
> I can hear the book telling stories
> I can hear the pencil drawing a car
> I can hear the tape recorder turning itself on

and another dictates to the same teacher:

> My friend shares food.
> My friend shares biscuits.
> My friend shares toys.
> My friend shares with me.

116

My friend plays ring - a - ring - a - roses
My friend plays sticky toffee
My friend plays it.
My friend plays with me.

My friend helps me when I trip over.
My friend helps me to get up.
My friend helps me to tidy up.
My friend helps me.

My friend is kind in the swimming pool.
My friend is kind in the playground.
My friend is kind in the classroom.
My friend is kind to me.

I quoted a vigorous example in my earlier book (Sedgwick 1997a):

I wish I could paint the stamping rocks
and the squeaking birds
and the juicy orange
the twisting keys
and ticking clock
and jumping blood
smashing egg
the ringing bell
and slamming gates
splashing sauce
yawning man
crashing sea
the twirling fish

(nine year old)

Barrs (1987) is right when she says that 'when listing is recognised as an important mental activity and is encouraged as a form of writing, young children can use lists as a way of setting down what they know. The lists can then form a framework for further enquiry'. I asked some six years olds for lists that would tell me what they would do on Christmas morning, and one wrote:

I
am
wack
my
dad

up
and
I
will
go
down
stairs

and so on, reminding us yet again that what we send across from our side of the bridge to the child's side is never received in exactly the same form as when we sent it. This is not a matter of a child misunderstanding, of being stupid, but of her hearing the word 'list' and immediately making connections relevant to her: a sight of a shopping list, for example, or a Christmas card list. It points up a crucial point about language, whether spoken or written: that the receiver, whether hearer or reader inevitably, in the nature of things, has a creative relationship to the speaker's or writer's utterance. Most of us find it easier to misquote than to quote correctly, because we are all, in small or large ways, creative individuals aching to make things our own. In any case, as Wilde said, anyone can quote accurately, but he quoted with great feeling. This child is responding with her experience.

We can look at older children writing about their early childhood to learn. These ten year olds have listened twice to Thomas Hood's famous poem 'I remember' ('I remember, I remember,/The house where I was born,/The little window where the sun/Came peeping in at morn'). Children are full of memories, and have a sure sense of nostalgia, of the physical facts that recall to us a whole scene. Here the poignant refrain of Hood's poems has set them free remembering with great power. Also, these older writers are using the list genre to make their poems:

> I remember I remember
> sitting outside at night
> watching the garden,
> bats, moon, stars and light.
> I remember I remember
> the bottom of that very dark garden
> sitting on the patio in the chair.
> with Mum and Dad
> drinking my milk.
> I remember I remember
> the dark-tasting night.
>
> Owen

I remember I remember
The hospital room,
The smell of the food,
The visitors, they were talking . . .
I remember I remember
The oxygen mask that I kept
Pushing off my face.
I remember I remember
All the nice doctors and nurses.
I remember I remember
Going through a tunnel that we
Used to call Hatfield Tunnel.
I remember I remember
Coming home to a house I did not remember.

Rachel

Other excerpts:

I remember I remember
my Grandad holding me
in his giant wrinkly old hand

Rebecca

I remember I remember
when I had just had a bath
and my Dad wrapped me
inside a towel
and I sat on his knee
and blew bubbles

Emma

The simple idea of lists linked to Hood's poem has produced some memorable phrases: 'Coming home to a house I did not remember' made one teacher gasp because, I reflected later, it describes an experience adults simply cannot have, unless mentally damaged by disease or accident; an adult who had had that experience would not have been able to write about it. The child who writes 'the bottom of that very dark garden/sitting on the patio in the chair/with Mum and Dad/drinking my milk' creates an almost universal image, and 'the dark-tasting night' in its context is vivid and scary. These children are celebrating love in their early years – the memories of parents and grandparents. They are also exposing with chilling honesty what Drummond (1993) has called 'the emotional turbulence' of their lives. One ten-year-old girl wrote:

I remember I remember
coming out of school and not going to our road
but going to St Michael's Road instead
and I said to my Mum Why are we going here
and she said Do you want Peter to be your new dad
and I said yes so he was.

8

SOME MECHANICS

In this chapter, I address secretarial issues in children's writing, especially spelling.

Literacy hour

A note, first, about the literacy hour. The National Literacy Project was set up in 1996 to 'raise standards of literacy in primary schools in line with national expectations and to meet the Government's targets by the year 2002 by improving the school's [*sic* – not the teachers'] management of literacy through target setting linked to systematic planning, monitoring and evaluation by headteachers, senior staff and governors; setting clear expectations bench-marked in a term-by-term structure'. Later, in January 1998, David Blunkett, the Secretary of State for Education, told teachers that work on literacy should be increased by one hour a day, and other subjects should be reduced.

This all ignores the fact that language figures in every part of our learning, of every part of our life. We can't study geography or history without talking and writing about it. In these pronouncements by governments, we see a view of language as something you must learn, before you can use it well, instead of something you learn by using it. More importantly, we are concerned with control again, rather than the child's autonomy, with passive rather than active learning. Control is a central issue when we discuss what are today called the 'basics' in language, as we will see from the following. I would argue that a child discussing death and life and love is engaged on something far more basic than a child checking a spelling, or copying a list of words in the decontextualised setting of the literacy hour.

Spelling: the historical context

John Hart, writing in 1569, bemoaned the 'disorders and confusions' of spelling that were so great that 'there can be made no perfite Dictionarie nor

121

Grammer'. His contemporary, Shakespeare, notoriously spelt his own surname in different ways. Anthony Burgess (1992) tells us in his absorbing, eccentric book on language that 'during the English Renaissance ... there was no agreed spelling, and this enabled the speaker of English to spell as he pronounced, or thought he pronounced'. He tells us that printers, needing to justify a line – that is, make the right-hand margin straight like the left-hand one – would add letters to words to fill the line out to the required length, making 'dog', for example, 'dogge', and 'not' to 'notte', or even 'noughtte'. Standardisation of spelling, with Samuel Johnson's Dictionary, didn't come until the eighteenth century.

But now spelling is seen as very important: Czerniewska (1992) says that we pay 'disproportionate attention to our own and other people's spelling inadequacies'. Most teachers have, on occasions, shown parents a piece of writing by their young child that, the teacher thought, expressed vividly some feeling, or some knowledge, or even some love, only to be asked, 'But what about her spelling – it's terrible'. The reasons given for this high status are supposed to be concerned with communication, but it has to be said that few readers would have much difficulty reading 'anemal' as 'animal', 'acomodation' as 'accommodation', or 'rite' as 'right'. The real reason for an obsession with spelling is because a good speller with no imagination can always correct an artist or scientist working at top pressure, even though that artist or scientist has an imagination capable of moving mountains. Or, as Harold Rosen put it in conversation with Donald Graves (1983) 'Any idiot can tell a genius he has made a spelling mistake'. Less bluntly, Frank Smith (1982) puts it like this: 'ability to spell [is] certainly not a reliable indicator of the fluency or creativity of the writer'.

In other words, correcting someone's spelling is a glib way of establishing a cheap superiority over him or her. Cheap, because to be good at spelling is easier than to understand Joyce's *Ulysses* or Stephen Hawking's *A Brief History of Time*, or to be a good mother or a good teacher. And we might note that many people who have been told they are bad spellers are self-conscious about the fact, and emphasising it causes needless distress. In fact, spelling obsessives do far more harm than they know, especially if they are working in classrooms with young children. Mark came to school aged five, never having questioned for a moment the fact that he is a writer. He had filled pages of paper with scribble, and read the stories he says they tell to his parents, who have always expressed interest in them. When he was very young, a different story would be told with the same scribble on the same day; but one day, a moment came when he realised that a story always says (in a limited sense, anyway) the same thing.

So Mark, when he comes to school, writes MJK for magic and MS for mouse, because he has found that consonants are relatively trustworthy, and he is good with (and fond of) the letter M because of his own first name. Another example of this invented spelling is John (in Graves 1983) who writes SSKT for This is a truck.

But when Mark is in Year 2, a spelling obsessive corrects every single one of his mistakes. She confronts him with dark looks. She surrounds words in his precious work with red circles and lines. She converts him inside a fortnight (and remember, she is a teacher) from a writer into a non-writer. Mark has grasped and then internalised, with shocking suddenness, the lie that writing and spelling are the same thing. So he understands another lie: that, since he can't spell right, he can't write right either. And, to rub salt into this wound, the teacher doesn't help Mark with his spelling crimes. All she does is to tell him, in the most cursory way, that he has committed them. Later, when he is nine, Mark writes, 'My pensl get al splig rog'.

Something has happened here: there is, after all, more than one way to abuse a child. This way of abusing makes spelling everything. As Drummond (1998) puts it

> Starting with children would entail . . . recognising their powers. It would mean abandoning our tendency to focus on children's weaknesses and incapacities, as evidenced in hundreds of items in baseline assessment schedules that record what children cannot do, or do not seem to know. It would mean recognising that all children learn, that learning is what they do best, and that they have been doing it from birth.

Graves (1983) tells us that 'When children come to school about ninety percent believe they can write. Only fifteen percent believe they can read.' The teacher's job is to build on this confident assumption about writing, not to destroy it.

So teacher- and parent-perfectionists in spelling destroy, rather than encourage, writers. Anyone who has written at any level above shopping lists knows that you have to live with possible errors while the thought process is taking you forward in terms of meaning. I have a poem about men cleaning the outsides of windows of a classroom where I was teaching. It has the word 'buddleia' in it, but at the point where I had to write it down, two things happened: one was that I realised I couldn't spell it, at least not with any confidence; and second, I realised that I had some ideas coming up. So, concerned that I might forget about these before I got to the place where I had to use them, I wrote something like 'buddl—— -a' and carried on, checking with the dictionary later.

Stalin County Primary

I know one infant school where I suggested the children did this. A modern building next to an Victorian junior school, it is very attractive in more significant ways, and it wouldn't take an OFSTED inspector or government minister to find it so. It's in a working-class area near a big city. Once you're inside you notice that children's paintings are displayed with a rare verve.

Many of them, for example, are in clipframes, and others are displayed double- or triple-mounted against attractive, often hessian, backgrounds. The school (I later discover) has three computers in each classroom, and there is no problem finding a word processor ready to go, with an attached (and this is rare) working printer.

After an hour or so in the school, you begin to notice that there is a certain style in the display of pictures: paper pinned on the wall arranged with care, and already printed with children's designs; and on this uniform background there are arranged drawings – good ones – of self-portraits, or machines closely observed, or of African masks, or flowers. Slightly oddly, the spacious staffroom has net curtains. And you notice something else that is more to the purpose of this book. There are countless examples of children's writing on the walls, also decorated with mounts and borders. But they are all spelt perfectly. Is this because the children in this area all spell perfectly when they come?

In a lunchtime meeting, the deputy headteacher makes something clear to me. The school's policy says that children must check that their spelling is correct in a wordbook before they write the word down in their notebook. This troubles me, first because I am to lead an INSET session after school, second because (as has become clear, I hope, in this book) I always try to treat schoolchildren as autonomous, active writers. I suggest to the deputy (the head is away) that children are 'emergent writers'; that, whether we see them as such, this is a fact of life; and that I am going to have to raise this in the INSET session. She says: 'We don't mind what the teachers *talk about*, as long as they don't *do* it . . . our English policy is non-negotiable.'

I would not have raised this question except for an experience I've had in the first class I've taught. They're older infants, and one child, Eleanor, says magical things in response to my questions. When I ask her to write them down, she says 'I can't write'. Why am I so disappointed by this? I often say I can't sing, I can't draw, I can't dance, I can't swim, I can't do maths. Well, I know that at some point I was taught that I can't do these things. When I was about twelve a maths master tousled my hair as I wept over a quadratic equation (or something) 'Don't you worry Sedgwick, just get on with your essays'. Comforted as I was then, I found it difficult to forgive later, as my failure in maths hardened into permanence, to the point where my eye has learnt to slide over figures in novels, and statistics mean nothing to me. I had been an emergent mathematician. I have been an emergent draftsman, an emergent dancer and an emergent swimmer. But now I can do none of these things, and this is in part because of a teacher.

Eleanor is an emergent writer. It doesn't matter, as far as that definition is concerned, whether the writers of her school's language policy see her as such or not. She began composing when her thinking got to the point when she began to order her thoughts in her brain, and she began writing when she began scribbling. Her school's policy may decide whether her writing is allowed to go on emerging, or whether it will have to go over certain hurdles, the highest of which is having to check the spellings of words. And as I reflect on this child, all my earlier observations of this school click into place: the displays, the certain style of pictures. This school is concerned with control. It is a middle-class enclave controlling, first, working-class children, and second, the young teachers who, by and large, staff the place.

The check-spellings-first policy explains why, in this classroom, there forms around the teacher and myself two word queues – or, because both of us are constantly moving around the classroom to help the decreasing number of children still in their places, word congas. I suspect that, if I had time to examine this conga over a few minutes, I might well find that the child in the third place is always the same child, using her native wit to avoid work, and that there is, behind her, a child who wants to know how to spell 'Ferrari', unaware that I won't be able to help.

The young teachers in this school require some thought, because a school is concerned not merely with children, but also with teachers. Unfashionable as the phrase sounds, each school is *a community of learners*. And to say that 'we don't mind what they talk about as long as they don't do it' is disrespectful to the point of an educational Stalinism: one can imagine Uncle Jo remarking cynically during the dark days of the 1930 purges 'I don't care what the poets talk about in their little flats, but I won't let them publish anything'. A school's management has a responsibility, it seems to me, not just to the children in its care, but also to the teachers and their development; to their freedom to think and practise.

Also, the management of this school seems to break Wells' principles (p. 21): it is not paying attention to what the children say as they write, but to how they write it; it is not trying to understand the children, and therefore cannot take the child's meaning as a basis for what to say next, or of the child's ability to understand. It is not paying attention to the children, but to their mistakes, all of which have enough publicity already, in league tables and political speech.

Development of spelling skills

To a greater or lesser extent, all adults have learned to live with uncertainty and discrepancy. The major themes of our life – love, work, reading, holidays, religion, politics, illness, schoolwork – end each day, not with a resounding major chord, but in a state of provisionality because, as Alain Robbe-Grillet said somewhere, *les choses ne sont jamais définitivement en ordre*. I press the save key on this book each night knowing something has been crudely expressed, and must be worked on in the morning. What I have written (and, eventually, what I publish) is, as Robert Frost says of a poem, only a 'temporary stay against confusion'. Nothing has ever completely resolved for a religious person the apparent gap between the love of God and the death of innocent children, or for any of us the gap between expectation and reality.

125

Even at the low level of spelling, this provisionality is difficult, because we like things to look good and be right, but it has to be lived with and even celebrated if we are to become autonomous writers. Indeed, truth is most likely to be found in the pursuit of discrepancy. Needing to be correct straightaway distorts what we have to say, because we are tempted to find a word we can spell instead of a more vivid one, one that carries the action further, or adds to the atmosphere, or moves the reader. Nearly all teachers have asked children to find 'a better word than nice' when writing; indeed, I once saw a list on the wall of a classroom that offered the children twenty or so such words: 'pleasant, agreeable, tasty, kind . . .'. But teachers who demand correct spelling at the point of composition must expect nice, because it is easy to spell.

There is a politics of correct spelling. It is, obviously, about control. Much as a teacher can control a child's perception and progress in narrative by restricting the child to a graded reading scheme, so the teacher can control a child's writing by demanding correct spelling in the first draft. Thus we have the word queue, comprising some children who are keen to get on with what they are about to write, but who can't, because they don't know how to spell 'Alton Towers' or 'Pleasurewood Hills' or 'Ferrari'; these children actually want to do the task they've been asked to do – write about a good day during the summer, say, or a ride in a rich relative's car – but instead have to, because of a school law, spend time by the desk, waiting.

Over-emphasis on spelling, which is a surface, rather than a substantive feature, of writing, at the expense of content, is a way of controlling what, when and how children write (and, therefore, think). As Czerniewska (1992) writes, 'spelling . . . is more than linguistically important, it is socially important . . . While the social attitudes cannot be ignored, they need to be recognised and put in perspective.'

Children's attempts at spelling (wrong to the spelling obsessive's eyes) at various stages are often evidence of learning, much as we interpret early speech such as 'I have runned' as evidence of understanding regular verbs, rather than as mistakes.

At the pre-literate stage, children, having recognised that they are surrounded by print that communicates, imitate that print with scribbles. Even now, sixteen years after his birth, I wish I had been a better audience for the scribbles my son made when he was small.

Soon after this, children begin to show an awareness of phonic principles: 'wndo clner' for window cleaner is one example on my desk, from a five year old. There seems little point in reacting to this other than with encouragement. Certainly to put a red ring round all such efforts is more likely to kill off the writer in a child at a stroke than to encourage that writer.

An understanding of phonetics increases as the child begins to see that sounds are represented by letters. Here we get the kind of spelling that English would have had it not descended so gloriously, if confusingly, from so many different languages. The children write 'windo kleener' and 'hej'. Later still, children move from phonic dependence, to seeing that words can look right, too.

Spelling is always second in priority to the content, to what the child is attempting to tell the reader. Merely to use a second draft to correct spelling (and, come to that, to correct punctuation and grammar) is, as Graves (1983) has put it, 'to manicure the corpse'. But spelling has to be taught.

Strategies for teaching spelling

Correcting children's spelling is, in its place, a useful activity. What is worse than useless is to put correcting marks on every wrong word in a piece of writing. However, a seven year old with advanced writing competencies should have certain words corrected. These are words that the child uses a good deal; in a sentence like 'I whent to Altn Tawers', it is probably a good idea, on most occasions, to correct 'whent' and, less certainly, 'Tawers', while leaving 'Altn' alone as a word the child probably won't want for a while. The crucial element here is that the words should be corrected at the child's side, and be put in the context of what the child is trying to do: to communicate.

It seems vital, too, that correcting a child's draft should never concentrate solely, or even largely, on spelling. If the piece is readable, first comments should always be about the content, just as any response to children talking should concentrate on what they say rather than on any impediments in their delivery. Such comments would, in fact, be appalling manners: blanket red-inking of children's writing is appalling manners, too, or worse.

Some writers have long advocated linking handwriting with spelling. This implies that it is useful for children to learn certain common strings of words, such as 'ear', 'ough', 'ean' and 'ar', and to write them from the beginning in joined-up script. This is what the children at Tacolneston do. As the school's handwriting policy says, they 'present work in a variety of ways, with a fluent, neat, cursive script'. Children can also be taught a simple drill: look, cover, remember, write, check. The teacher writes the correct spelling down. The child looks. The word is covered. The child tries to remember, and writes her memory of the correct spelling down, then checks whether she has got it right.

Having a go

This seems to me to be very important, because it's how writers work. It's what I was doing when I tried to spell 'buddleia'. Even very young children can do this, with their strings of often capital consonants.

Using the spellchecks

Children are going to grow into their adolescence and adulthood with information technology that we as teachers cannot conceive of. For the

127

purposes of this chapter, it needs to be said that the spellcheck on the word processor should become a tool in the hands of children which they use readily. One headteacher told me that the spellchecker 'de-skills' children, much as a calculator de-skills them: a less puritanical way of looking at this would be to say that both tools take out some of the chore element in writing and mathematics, and leave space for the creative.

A note about handwriting

Why just a note? As Browne (1993) insists, handwriting is the servant, never the master when children are writing, and an over-emphasis on it, like an over-emphasis on spelling, can destroy the potential writer in a child. I watched in fascinated discomfort as a child in a poetry lesson worked for half a minute on an apparently perfect italic 'The' before erasing it and starting again. The school management, with its emphasis on presentation and the italic style, not to mention display, had taught him to do this. It was, wittingly or otherwise, controlling the child: while he was getting the look of a word as immaculate as someone who was teaching needed it to be he was not making anything new.

One simple means of enabling children to distinguish between the content of a piece of work (which this child should have been concentrating on here) and the presentation (which he was, in fact, concentrating on, though to the serious detriment of there being any work at all worth speaking of) is to discourage the use of erasers. They present children, and therefore the teacher, with several problems. First, like a DELETE key on a word processor, they encourage the loss of material that the writer may need again later. Second, if a child-writer is inclined for some reason to waste time, the eraser is a perfect excuse. Third, and far more important, erasers give the child a dishonest message: that anything can be perfect on the first writing-out. It is far better for children to cross errors out neatly so that they are still visible: they may turn out not be errors after all.

Joined-up handwriting from the beginning, as I have said, is currently being presented as an answer to spelling problems. As well as this, it helps fluency and is consistent with most adult handwriting practice. Is such an approach from the beginning compatible to a developmental approach to writing? I agree with Browne (1993) that there are problems here. She says:

> To expect children to move from pre-literate marks on paper to joined-up writing would exclude the other stages that children go through as they are learning about the writing system. The use of capitals plays a part in spelling development when children use letter names . . . [Also], as the typeface in children's books is usually print script, to introduce joined-up writing from the start would seem to be at variance with the models children see.

Browne goes on to suggest that there are problems when children join up before they can form letters correctly. I accept her advice that the less rigid system of using exit strokes from the start is the best compromise here. For more practical help in this subject, I refer the reader to pages 79–83 of Browne's (1993) excellent primer on helping children to write.

The skills needed in handwriting are developed through a wide variety of exercises in art and play. More specifically, drawing from the earliest years might be more significant in developing the kind of free, easy movement that is useful in handwriting. Drawing is, also more importantly, a good preparation for writing, as the mind can be set free to think.

Part III

CHILDREN AND READING

9

FACING PRINT

In this chapter I discuss reading. I place it in a position behind mark-making and talking because, like the human race, children are makers of marks before they are interpreters of them. I suggest that the literacy industry is less concerned with the autonomy of the child than with two related and less honourable factors: managerial/political control of teacher and child stemming from the current political hegemony on the one hand and, on the other hand, profit. There is also a glimpse of Reading Recovery at work.

Why have I left reading till last? First, because, as I have written with my wife elsewhere, the human race was from the beginning a mark-making race. Mark-decoding, obviously, came later:

imagine a drawing on a cave wall: a roughly made boar, perhaps, with a spear sticking out of it and two humans staring at it . . . They know this drawing is telling them something and they have a dim idea of what it might be . . . what is it about? religion, food, celebrations, magic. Now the mark has been made, they have to puzzle it out, to interpret it . . . But, conversely, with our children we treat reading (which is interpreting and decoding) as the primary act.

(Sedgwick and Sedgwick 1993)

Second, though I may seem to have devalued reading by giving it a position so late in my book, I emphasise that it is implicit and alive in everything I have written so far, especially in Chapters 4–8 on writing. It is often forgotten that children read organically (that is, they read widely, without being asked to, advertisement hoardings, television screens, sweet wrappers, pub and shop signs and all sorts of logos and badges). With enormous variations in fluency, accuracy and enthusiasm, reading grows. It is also forgotten that children read not only what has been written to seduce them into consumption or to train them as phonetic decoders: *they also read their own writing*. This writing is an untapped resource in many schools, where teachers haven't noticed, possibly, that writers can be encouraged to check frequently what they have written by reading it over, even aloud, or at least moving their lips, to themselves.

This procedure – children reading their own and each others' writing – can be of double benefit to children. First, it helps them to develop and enrich what they have written. Seamus Heaney has commented that poems don't appeal only to the senses of sight (on the page) and hearing (when read out), but to the sense of taste; therefore he reads his poems to himself half-aloud, whispered not vocalised. This is good advice for children: move your lips as you read what you have drafted. Second, and more to the immediate point of this part of my book, this procedure helps children to practise their reading. Children can read each other's writing with enjoyment and more purpose than they can many a reading scheme book.

A critique of the literacy industry

On 12 September 1997, *The Times Educational Supplement* published a 'guide to literacy projects' in which Maureen O'Connor attempted a summary of seventeen publications. Some were classroom-based schemes; others supplied 'help with phonics'; the third group were concerned with promoting reading. I wrote to all the publishers, and what follows is an attempt to build a critique of the burgeoning literacy industry based on what these publishers sent me. Four questions emerged in my thinking as I tried to evaluate the material that I had been sent.

First, was there any evidence that children had been consulted? There was an easy, short answer here: there wasn't. One wonders why the writers of projects and schemes designed to help children to take 'first steps', 'extend literacy' and 'recover' from early failure (to use three fashionable phrases from this material) never ask the children for their view on reading, and their experiences of how they learnt to read. I have mentioned several times Wells' basic rules for assessing children's language (see pp. 21ff.). They were broken time and time again here. This seems to me, once again, to show a lack of respect for children: their selves, their experiences, their aspirations. I suppose the assumption behind this neglect of children's perspectives is based on the conventional view of children as know-nothings, or at least no-littles.

But young children will readily offer answers to questions such as 'How did you read that word?' such as 'I knew the first letter' or 'I looked at the picture'. I asked some six year olds about words they were reading:

> I read 'excited' because it has an 'x' in it . . . 'kitchen' because it has a 'ch' in it . . . 'traffic' because it has a 'tra' in it . . . 'adventurous' because it has 'adventure' in it.

Illustration 22

'blurred' has got an 'e' and a 'd' in it [looking at a picture in a book about glasses, a view of a street seen by someone with short sight] and the picture is fuzzy . . . 'carefully' . . . Ben's in there with breaky things, things mustn't break, he's carrying them carefully.

There is no reason why children should not also have ready, useful and pointed answers to questions about reading books and schemes in general. There is a need for research in this area and, if it has already been done, some news about it.

Second, was the material commercially produced or was it the result of a more altruistic initiative? This is not meant to suggest that all commercial materials for schools are less useful than other materials. But I am sure that the profit motive has its usual implications for classroom use. For example, I found, unsurprisingly, that such material was glossy and slickly produced, and, at the same time, less likely to recommend books outside their publisher's catalogue. It was also less likely to show awareness of the need for books for children to fit into context: their lives, their affections, their interests and schooling. This criterion assumed a significance for me in that I have felt for a long time that those of us involved in schools have an insufficiently critical stance towards the catalogues that the publishing industry aims at us.

Third, were teachers involved in the research and development of the material? For some years, I have seen teachers as professionals on a continuum: at one end of it, they are hardly teachers at all, but mere hired hands implementing someone else's syllabus. That someone might be a politician or an inspector or a headteacher. It might be the representative of an organisation or a commercial publisher. It might, indeed, be someone representing a government or a regime. Increasingly since the late 1970s teachers have become less involved in the designing of curricula, in the decision-making about what should happen in the classroom.

At the other end of the continuum, there are teachers who, in spite of everything that has been done to them since the late 1970s, are professional in the fullest sense: they, or colleagues they have confidence in, have had a significant role in preparing and evaluating the curriculum they teach. This is related to the two previous criteria: professionals developing schemes will, first, involve children, teachers and their opinions; second, they will examine commercial material in the light of children's and teachers' views.

Finally, did the scheme appear to live in any context? Was it, in other words, rooted in what Drummond (1998) calls the 'emotional turbulence' of children's lives, in stories and poems written for children, and in the rest of the curriculum?

How did these materials answer these questions?

Jolly Phonics can stand for other entirely sound-based schemes. It was 'perfected' (a large, shameless claim made in the publicity material) 'over two decades in a Suffolk primary school . . . it involves the use of phonic flash-cards . . . early reading scheme books and daily diaries'. Apparently, it was developed by two teachers, though whether they did any research with colleagues is not recorded. There was no joyful, pleasurable flirtation in Jolly Phonics with 'real' books or 'multi-layered texts' (Watson 1993). The books used were produced solely by Jolly Learning Ltd, and if there was a vested interest, it wasn't in introducing children to the world of literature.

The images in the catalogue – snakes, mice and bees grinning and smirking – were twee, and contrasted with the vigour of other images young children will have come across at this stage: picture books by Shirley Hughes, David McKee, Anthony Browne and Babette Cole, to take four examples at random among hundreds on my, and my son's, shelves. Learning was sheered off in this scheme from any available contexts: children's lives, the world of literature, the rest of the infant school curriculum were as evident as requited love in a brothel. Inorganic, planted on the child's experience, Jolly Phonics contained pages that (as one teacher in her early forties put it to me) 'were just like the books I remember learning to read from'. If, as seems to be widely agreed by politicians and inspectors, these pages did not work for enough children, one wonders why they are being wheeled out again with their air of rarefied, trivial tweeness?

This scheme would suit the writer I quoted on p. 61, who condemned 'hot gospellers, livid with intolerant enthusiasm' (in other words, they saw broader views of the teaching of reading). Such simplistic thinking like Turner's is useful for politicians who want to condemn teachers, because if teaching reading can be sold to a simple tabloid press as a simple set of simple skills, pinning the rap on schools is a simple matter. Creators of schemes like Jolly Phonics ignore the fact that, as Fox (1993: 28) puts it, 'Some children internalise the patterns and structures of written language well before the acquisition of independent literacy.'

I had been sent details of the National Literacy Project. This was marked for me by the managerial language that has infected education since the late 1970s. With its emphasis on 'national expectations', 'evaluation by headteachers and senior staff', 'audits', 'monitoring' and 'targets', this rhetoric effectively sidelines teachers and places them in the 'hired hand' category. Teachers are not, in the world of the National Literacy Project, researchers and developers, or even involved in research and development; they are creditors at 'banks of ideas'; they are audiences to approved 'individual teachers . . . identified as . . . models'. One sentence leaped off the page: 'The strategy for implementation is a "cascade" model so every link in the chain needs to be as robust as possible.' With its ringing mixed metaphor and its assumption of cowed passivity on the part of the teachers, this tells us all we need to know about the status of teachers in this new world. My book, in contrast, is predicated on the assumption that teachers should be, and still can be, active learner-professionals.

The literacy hour contrasts with my emphasis in another way. I have tried to show that, to paraphrase a car window sticker, literacy is for life, not for an hour; not just for that part of the day we aren't teaching geography, history, music, art or physical education. The easy, populist notion of an hour for literacy flies in the face of human experience, where all of us, including children, are bombarded with print during most waking moments of our lives. To recognise that there are different purposes implicit in this print – to cajole, to make us buy, to make us laugh, to move us to tears, to express a truth, to badger us, communicate, to talk about love and hate, to engage us in the eternal struggle with words and meanings – is to recognise the inadequacy of a model of the printed word that sees the teaching of that word cocooned and disempowered inside a safe little reading scheme which has only one admitted purpose.

And, with targets and objectives, and the resultant model's constant emphasis on what children are failing at, and on what they should be rather than what they are, it also contrasts with my emphasis on what children are capable of and successful at, and on what they are doing now. Objectives are also open to other criticisms. As I have written before:

> they do not cater for learning in the areas where there are serious questions to be asked; they tend, therefore to narrow learning to the odds and sods that can be measured; that they tend, because of that tendency, to make teaching banal.
>
> (Sedgwick 1993)

Other projects described in the *TES* article contrasted with these. For example, the University of Exeter's Extending Literacy Project developed a process model, thus refocusing our attention on the children as they are as we teach them, rather than on what they ought to be or have, in the past, failed to be. Its writers see literacy as more than 'a mastery of the "basics"' of reading. The model the project uses includes 'activation of previous knowledge', a component emphasised in practical terms by Wells (1986) and the other writers I have quoted, but absent in, for example, Jolly Phonics, which assumes ignorance rather than previous knowledge.

Reading Recovery: a glimpse

What follows is an adapted version of an article I wrote for *The Times Educational Supplement* (25 January 1991).

'Ian, you're brilliant! . . . Good boy!' This six year old is beginning his daily one-to-one session with his Reading Recovery teacher. He's been coming to these special lessons since April 1990 when his authority, Surrey, launched the scheme. I watch as he writes familiar words. He gets his name correct ('I like the way you've written that!' says his teacher) and then he chooses 'my' – and gets that right too. ('Well done Ian.') When he writes 'cad' for 'cat', his teacher smiles 'Ian, I like the way you *began* that word.'

Ian is here in what Reading Recovery enthusiasts call the 'roaming around the known' phase of his half-hour lesson. His teacher is building his confidence by emphasising constantly what he can do. Then, as Ian reads aloud, he makes several mistakes. The teacher corrects none of them. Instead, she marks a sheet of paper discreetly with ticks and crosses, building up data for a diagnostic analysis. She is constantly positive and energetic. The lesson moves at a tearaway speed: 'Let's do these letters – ready, steady, go!' There is no time for what Jean Prince, Surrey's advisory teacher for Reading Recovery, calls trivia.

It was Jean Prince, a former primary headteacher, who trained Ian's teacher in Reading Recovery (RR). She had spent 1989 at the Reading Recovery Centre at the University of Auckland where the scheme was developed. 'I am totally committed to it. I know it's expensive in the early stages, but it will save so much in the long term.' The expense that Jean Prince mentions is largely for supply cover, and also the teacher training, which comprises half a day a year. There is also a nucleus of materials: books, magnetic board and letters, and travel. Almost all the children are 'accelerated' (a RR word) to average reading scores when they 'exit' (another RR word) from the project.

Jean Prince says that this rate of success depends on four factors. First, an early start (the pupils chosen for the programme are the lowest achieving six year olds). Second, it is intensive: half an hour every day for as long as the child needs (normally between 12 and 20 weeks). Third, Reading Recovery helps the child discover strategies of his or her own. Fourth, above all, it accentuates the positive. Marie Clay, who developed the programme, noted how many remedial teachers concentrated on the failings of their children – and thus exacerbated them.

In the programme, the children are withdrawn from their class. Doesn't this run counter to post-Warnock trends in British special needs thinking? Barbara McGilchrist, of the Institute of Education in London, says no – as long as the project is seen as part of the school's language policy, not a 'bolt-on'. Also 'liaison between the class teacher and the Reading Recovery teacher is vital'.

In the next chapter I discuss Reading Recovery (and other methods) in terms of the politics of reading.

10

THE POLITICS OF READING

In this chapter, I follow Harry Daniels (1993), placing the teaching of reading in its often ignored political context. I then describe and discuss the theory and practice of Liz Waterland (1986) as an example of a school that openly takes a political stand; that is, a stand which involves giving children choice.

Thinking about children reading involves thinking about what human beings always have been, what (most importantly) they are and what they might become. This, not understood by politicians, inspectors and institutions like OFSTED (with their larger concerns), is true of all (I choose these two words carefully) training and education. Are children destined to become hired labourers in a society that values individual freedom very little (training)? Or are they, on the other hand, to become participants in a democracy (education)? Deciding whether we should train or educate children is a political decision.

Most of us make decisions about schools without ever verbalising the politics of them, or the politics of the system in which they exist. Indeed, many of us are offended at the very notion that we are political beings at all, or dwellers in a political context. Three days after the 1997 general election a headteacher told me, in answer to my question about the boundaries of the constituency in which her school stood, 'I don't get involved with the politics.' But this unawareness of – and, indeed, hostility to – the politics of educational decisions serves only to make the politics all the stronger because, by disguising the political hegemony as common sense, we make it invisible.

Czerniewska (1992) says, 'There is no "autonomous" model of literacy – it is shaped by politics and ideology.' It is a 'socially constructed phenomenon'. She means (I take it) that there is no way of looking at literacy in an objective, simple way. Politicians who use common sense as a way of making decisions are behaving disingenuously. In Victorian schools it was common sense to put

140

a failing child in the corner with a dunce cap on his or her head. As recently as the 1960s, in my experience, it was considered common sense to slipper disobedient boys (though not, usually, girls). It is still common sense in some schools that effervescent children should be 'crushed' before they can be taught anything.

Politics is essentially about who controls a given society; about who decides what autonomous model has power; and about who is to be controlled and who is in control. This politics becomes explicit when we talk about children and reading. If we control what children read through reading schemes and colour-coded libraries, we are teaching them that they do not have power over what they read; we are preparing them to be passive receivers of whatever is and will be put in front of them. We are treating them as nothing more than potential workers who will need to have certain skills in the business of decoding letters and other linguistic symbols in order to take their place in the economy. An anecdote will provide a seed for much of our thinking in this area:

> A headteacher/parent of a nearly-four-year-old child: 'I was reading to her one of her bedtime books, and she said, "Mummy, why can't I read", and I brought home from school some early readers, and I started teaching her.'

Why couldn't the child learn to read on the books she was using at home, a book that she'd had some part in choosing from the shop or the library? This anecdote speaks to us about a distinction between learning (what you do when you toil over phonics) and pleasure (those stories and poems your parents read to you at bedtime, writing that excites, comforts and makes you think freshly about something).

In the section that follows, I discuss what Styles and Drummond (1993) call 'The Politics of Reading'. To begin with an analysis of my article on Reading Recovery, I suggest that the boy (Ian) is being controlled by unreconstructed behaviourist techniques. Accentuating the positive, humane, decent and sensible as it sounds, is little more than using positive reinforcers. It is manipulating a child and, much as the aims of the manipulations seem desirable, we must look at another side of our behaviour. There is what Daniels (1993) calls 'a fitness for purpose': we all want Ian and his friends to read successfully, but is there 'a fitness of purpose'?

As Daniels would put it, we have to ask where Ian is being placed on a dimension of dependence and independence. The control is firmly in the hand of the teacher. She is exclusively interested in Ian's deficits, and Ian knows this. The unerring, unremitting focus on those failures further disempowers him, as the teacher's expertise is moved like a battering ram against him. There is no focus on what he can do, on his emotional life, on his abilities in other areas like art or sport or science. There is, indeed, 'a close link between reading instruction and social control' (Whitehead 1993); while this is true in Ian's case, it is also true in the wider sense as children are measured against an over-simplified model of reading, and shown, at least to the satisfaction of the testers, to be failing.

Ian, and all those children, are being labelled; to identify failures early may sound like common sense because it enables remedial help to begin quickly, but it also condemns, possibly, children to a school career where less is expected of them. As many writers have said (Pollard and Tann 1993 for example) teachers are affected in their perceptions of children: sex, social class and race cause some of us to stereotype. At some point or other in most staffrooms we have taken part in a conversation containing the sentence 'He's called Wayne/Shane so I know he's trouble.' This labelling, dangerous as it is, can be exacerbated by the results of withdrawal and what is, effectively, remedial teaching.

Politics is present too in the way in which the reading debate is simplified. For example, seeing reading as a simple matter of matching sounds to characters makes it easy for politicians and the media to pin the rap of school failure on the teaching profession, which can thereby be seen as failing to do a simple thing well – or, indeed, at all. Also, seeing reading failure as simple legitimates the publication of grossly simplistic schemes like Jolly Phonics; legitimises, as it has legitimised for many years, the whole literacy industry, from Janet and John and The Gay Way, through Bangers and Mash, and the pirates Ben and Greg and Roderick, to the tiresome little noodles in the village with three corners. To see reading failure as more complicated – involving psychological and sociological factors and, of course the provision or lack of resources – makes it less useful as a political tool, and, of course infinitely more problematic.

Daniels (1993) argues persuasively that the various theories about how children learn to read are complex and, in fact, not understood by many teachers. The arguments become over-simplified and politicised; become, in fact, mere binary debates: real books versus reading scheme, look-and-say versus phonics and so on. He suggests that there is insufficient knowledge of how children learn to read, and that, therefore, reliance on one approach for all children is wrong. He mentions Dombey (1992), who argued caution over the sudden interest in Marie Clay's Reading Recovery methods, and who suggests that

> We should give time and money to help teachers develop a more rigorous classroom practice . . . In particular, this should include a real recognition of the experiences and expectations of literacy that children bring to school.

This is the sort of emphasis that I have made in earlier chapters, using the perceptions of Tizard and Hughes (1984) and Wells (1986).

Liz Waterland and the apprenticeship approach

There are approaches to teaching children reading that allow for, and even encourage, some autonomy; that assume that children are active learners, not empty jugs, blank sheets of paper or passive receivers of the wisdom of their elders. Liz Waterland (1986), the headteacher of Brewster Avenue Infant School in Peterborough and writer on the subject of children reading, says that 'It is not necessary, in fact it is counterproductive, to control the books children read, the words they read or the speed they progress at.' This remark can be appreciated better if seen in the living context of Waterland's school. To walk into it while it is empty of children is to walk into a huge, colourful tent of books. It speaks and teaches without a word being spoken, without any explicit instruction, of delight, of rhythm, of colour, of what the relationship of a reader with a book can, at its most potent, be. It teaches me as I wander through it. It speaks eloquently of choice. The teachers here seem aware of the fact that every serious act of choice in a school – Which book shall I read next? What shall I write about? Who shall I ask to listen to my new story? Who shall I tell about my new baby sister? – is of itself educational.

It isn't easy to build genuine choice into a school without worrying, for two broad reasons. First, the children may choose books or activities that the political hegemony – inspectors and politicians and other pundits of a moralistic and legalistic frame of mind – may have disallowed somewhere in their snowfall of paperwork or newsprint. Indeed, the very structure of an institution may well run counter to needs of its inmates for autonomy and freedom. A prison is an obvious example, a school a less obvious one. Second, the children may do things that we as teachers cannot see as valuable. They might want to talk about, or draw, or write about the current pop stars or cartoon favourites. They may write and in doing so break school rules about presentation: I have just seen one such set of rules pinned to a classroom wall, agreed by and applicable to, it proclaimed, all the schools in the area: 'All titles will be underlined. All writing will be dated . . . When writing is finished it will be ruled off . . . ' etc., etc. But 'love is proved in the letting go' said C. Day Lewis. And if we can't trust children, we can't educate them. Documents like this list of rules speak of control, not trust.

How is this choice of books made manifest to the children at Brewster Avenue Infants' School? When they come in at five years, every morning at 8.45, they face a long wide corridor from the front door, and what parts of the wall aren't covered with books are covered with children's pictures, or reproductions of art. Few of the books are displayed with their spines showing: most show off their front covers. Most of these books are what Watson (1993) calls 'multi-layered texts': texts 'which on subsequent readings yield more pleasure, or more significance, and enable the reader to experience a growing sense of delighted understanding and familiarity'. The multi-layered text is an organic text – one that grows as people read it, as people respond to it, and a school library that is composed of such texts is likewise organic. Someone or other knows that the library at Brewster Avenue contains all the Anthony Browne books, and that when there's a new one out, they must get that. The collection of books grows brightly alongside the children and their understanding of reading.

This is contrasted with a reading scheme text, which has one purpose only: to train a child in key words. It is a dead text that pretends to be a story. It is a dishonest corpse. 'Go Jon go. There is the dog. Here is the cat. It is black. Go Mary go. See the dog. Look at the cat. Is it black? Where is the cat? Where is the dog?' In her 1998 book, Waterland has a story about

> Robert [who] was reading from The Village with Three Corners scheme about the red door and the red roof and the red hat. When he had finished he looked at me. 'There's a bit missing' he said solemnly. 'Where's the bit what tells what happens?'

Even the best reading scheme texts leave the impression that a dead hand, remotely linked to a brain with tunnel vision, but utterly detached from a heart, has written them.

Brewster Avenue also has many books from different cultures and, although there are only two ethnic groups in the school – 'Peterborian and Italian', as Liz Waterland put it to me – a wide range of languages is represented on the shelves: Urdu, Mandarin, Italian, French as well as English. A multi-cultural approach, as Liz insists, is more important in school without ethnic minorities.

Waterland's (1986) book *Read With Me* is one of the most accessible and helpful contributions to the debate about children learning to read. She points out that the sterile, behaviourist model does not make readers, but decoders, a very different matter. She tells a chilling story:

> Paul . . . came . . . from another school . . . I asked, 'What were you reading at your last school, Paul?' 'Book Six', he said without enthusiasm. 'Book Six of what, Paul?' 'Dunno'. 'Well, who was in the story, what was it about?' I persisted. 'Dunno', he repeated. 'I don't think it was about anything, really. It was just Book Six'.

Anyone who has taught young children could tell stories like this. What did Paul think a book, or a story, or reading itself was? It was certainly not connected to pleasure or excitement, or any other rewarding emotion, as his computer, or his Action Man, or his football was. And Paul's perception of reading was not connected, either, to that image of an adult 'curled up', to use the conventional phrases, in an armchair 'with a good book', or absorbed late at night long after lights out with an adventure story. This mismatch between Paul's perception of reading, and our one – those of us who love books and,

Illustration 23

indeed, print of all kinds – can in no way be interpreted as a problem that comes from home, or from Paul's intellectual ability. It is a problem brought to Paul by the teachers he had before he went to Brewster Avenue.

Waterland outlines, in *Read With Me*, two approaches to teaching reading. The first one is the conventional approach, which I have already described implicitly in my paragraphs about Jolly Phonics. This approach is behaviouristic, and depends on a perception of reading as a hierarchy of skills which should be taught in bite-sized chunks until there is a 'total edifice of reading ability'. It depends on a view of reading (and, implicitly, the world and all its human behaviour) as orderly and logical, and ignores all experiences the children may have had before they come to school except what it dismissively calls 'pre-reading'.

In contrast, Waterland describes, in eight enlightening, liberating pages (pp. 13–19) her 'apprenticeship approach'. The basic difference between this and the conventional approach is that, while teachers using the latter see the demands of the text as working on largely passive children to get them to read, those using the apprenticeship model see children as working on the text, bringing to it all their previous experiences with words, sometimes explicitly, always implicitly. These experiences include, for example, moments when they have recognised their name on an envelope, or clamoured for a burger on seeing the McDonald's sign, or for a visit to the toy store on seeing the logo Toys 'R' Us. In these times, children are not the possessor of deficits, but of abilities they have generated themselves by interacting with their environment. Waterland has five propositions about children reading (see *Read With Me* for a fuller description of them); what follows is a summary.

The first proposition is that the acquisition of written language is comparable with that of spoken language. Waterland quotes Goodman (1982) who sees 'oral and written language as learned in the same way'. It would be over-simple (and wrong) to suggest that the child is learning the same skills; but the two sets of skills may be usefully compared. You wouldn't say to a baby gurgling 'I wish you'd stop trying to talk until you can do it properly.' We don't wait till children have certain skills before encouraging them to make their needs known. We don't even conceive of their talking, usually, as a matter of skill at all. You would accept that children learn to talk by imitation, by glimpsing increasingly the grammar that Chomsky says is inside their head, and by practice. Children learn to talk because of the light that is in their head, the light that lights everyone who comes into the world. Similarly, with help from the experts – parents and teachers and others – and (vitally) following their examples, children learn to read by reading.

The second proposition says that reading cannot be taught in a formal sequenced way any more than talk can. Life is a messy business, as anyone who's been in love, or lost a brother, sister, husband, wife, child or parent, or followed a team, must know. In both the serious and the trivial, there is glory and grief. Isn't life a terrible thing, thank God, as Dylan Thomas put it. The notion that children learn to read by amassing skills in a pre-ordained way is analogous to suggesting we should be taught how to fall in love, sustain that love, greet the death of our parents, and walk home cheerful after a home defeat, by the simple means of a life-skills curriculum. Folks who view life in such terms may, if pushed, after a glass or two, concede that it is a terrible and glorious thing, but will reduce it, when sober, insensately to a scheme. And a life-skills scheme will dictate that we shouldn't be allowed to progress to death till we deal with love. And till love till we'd dealt with life.

Third, and related to that, reading is not a sequence of small skills fluently used: it is a process of getting meaning. Notice how this proposition focuses on the notion of control: if reading is seen by the managers of a given school, or by the significant advisers or politicians, as a matter of tiny taught skills, teachers (or, more exactly, whoever has written the scheme they are teaching with, whoever is controlling that person) has complete control. If, on the other hand, reading is a matter of getting meaning, children control more and more of the setting as they bring to bear on it what they already know and partially understand. My son reading the words 'The Red Lion' for the first time is gaining meaning – obscure as it may be – about a place where he has sat in a garden with his parents, and where he may well sit again. Waterland quotes Marie Clay on this point: a child was discovered to be reading the text in columns rather than lines: 'Go, go, go, go. Tim up. Up Tim. Up, up, up.' 'Read from left to right' (says Waterland) 'the text became 'Go Tim. Go up. Go up Tim. Go up, up, up.' Waterland questions – rather too gently, as far as I am concerned – whether the second version makes any more sense than the first.

The fourth proposition is that the text we offer the child is crucial. That is the explanation for the warm, bright book-lined tent where the children cannot walk or run without confronting images in print and picture, and for the emphasis on books that set the mind thinking and feeling, rather than locking it into a prison cell, phonic or otherwise. When he was seven, my wife and I read *Treasure Island* to our son as his bedtime book. At the end of the story Jack Hawkins, the hero, is on a ship with a drunken villain, Israel Hands, from whom Jack has stolen a gun. Israel wakes from his stupor, feels for the missing gun, and staggers towards Jim. And Jim says: 'One step closer Mr Hands and I'll blow your brains out.' There was always a pause in the bedroom at this point. And then my son would say 'Can you read that bit again?' We are full of stories. We are obsessed by them. Feeding that obsession, that passion, when children are very young is arguably the most positive thing we can do in helping them to make themselves fluent readers.

The final proposition is that the role of the adult is to be a guiding friend. This will mean that the adult will not be an inquisitor, a tester; and she will not patronise the child for her small successes over letters and words. It will mean that she will sometimes read the book to the child, ask questions that are genuine ('What do you think will happen next?' and not 'Can you tell me this sound?'; 'Have you ever felt like that?' and not 'Have you forgotten that already?')

If you need a careful record of reading, see Waterland's *Read With Me* (p. 36).

11

REMEMBERING LEARNING
TO READ

How do children feel about learning to read? In this chapter, adolescents and adults of various ages talk about their memories.

Without scientific pretensions (I was not remotely rigorous about my samples, and the focus changed as I proceeded) I asked questions:

- Do you remember learning to read?
- Do you remember any difficulties?
- What books or other equipment was used?
- Who do you feel was most responsible for teaching you to read?

Bev (in her forties) helps to manage a small business in which the main worker is her husband, a blacksmith:

> I had Janet and John. I can't remember Mum or Dad reading to me. I caught on. Probably not really taught.

Pat jnr (blacksmith, in his forties)

> I can't remember . . . Janet and John, I think, but I honestly cannot remember . . . [When did you learn to read?] Last Thursday? . . . Most of it was difficult. I wasn't distressed, more embarrassed. There was no pre-nursery in those days. We were stuffed in the deep end. I can't remember much. School, I think, did most . . . I can't remember sitting down at home. I think I had the basic idea before I started . . . I can't remember.

Ruth (Pat jnr's mother, cook, in her sixties)

> I'm told that I learned to read, to read my letters off the sign, Parker's Ales, it was a pub then. My mum used to draw me pictures and I used

to copy them. My parents and me gran started me off. I used to sit up in bed and my gran used to read to me . . . In infants the teacher said a letter and you used to have to draw that letter on the board . . . No, I had no difficulties. I was clever you see! . . . You were terrified of the teachers of not getting it right.

Pat snr (Pat jnr's father, retired steel worker, in his sixties)

I could read before I went to school . . . I remember Enid Blyton's Sunny Stories . . . there was always books about. People higher up the school, that helped. Brothers and sisters, I was the youngest. There were comics about at home, *Beano*, *Wizard*. At school I don't remember . . . I thought I was born reading . . . but I've always been able to read!

Lucinda (photographer, in her fifties)

I was about 6 . . . Mum read to me, the Bible . . . the Honeycombs, Scripture Union, a booklet, there was a passage from the Bible and you had to do little puzzles. She always read them to me, and she would sing 'Jesus Tender Shepherd hear me, Bless thy little lamb tonight' . . . and then she'd turn the light off. I was terrified of reading aloud because the Bible was difficult. I remember lots of fear . . . It was easier at school because there were normal books, not Bible books . . . I remember Janet and John. The book has a cloth cover and it curled up at the edges, and we used to have book marks with coloured card and you wrote your name and your page number.

Brian (photographer, in his forties)

I don't remember a great deal . . . Janet and John . . . most of it happened at school. I have no memory of learning words with my mum and dad. There wasn't a houseful of books.

Glen (still at school, aged sixteen)

Mum kept telling me what the next word was . . . I was about five . . . I couldn't do it. I wanted to show I could, but I couldn't. I wanted to show off, show what a big boy I was. I used to get angrier and angrier and storm off. I felt stupid . . . I could read when I was about seven. It was more fun at school. Learning with friends. I didn't have to prove myself then, they were no better at it than I was.

Terry (window cleaner, in his early thirties)

> We'd stand up next to the teacher and read a couple of pages – Peter
> and Jane I think it was – and then she'd say, 'Can you read a couple
> of pages at home to Mum and Dad? . . . I'll know if you have, 'cos I'll
> be asking you about it!' . . . In the juniors it was those Pirate books .
> . . I'd no trouble reading . . . No I don't read now, I do maths and
> that . . . My daughter, we read to her about Rosie and Jim, and she
> makes her own little story up . . . She's three . . . and I reckon that's
> cleverer than reading it!

Colin (Baptist minister, in his fifties)

> I don't really remember much about it I don't really know what the
> answer to that question is. I remember mixing up my b's and d's, and
> the tall letters and the short letters.

Peter (a vicar in his forties) had unusually clear memories. Who had taught
him to read?

> My mother. We used to read lots of stories. I remember before I went
> to school there was a girl next door called Susan H—— and I
> remember lying on a floor writing the name by the sounds of the
> words . . .
> I remember at school one day I couldn't read the word 'oh', I was
> in the second year in the infants. Miss C—— was distracted and
> I moved the card down, pretending I had read 'oh' and she said when
> I got to her, 'We weren't there, we were there' and she moved the card
> back up . . . I could always read. When we were allowed to bring
> things into school, and the others brought cars or trucks, I always
> took a book in . . . I remember the flip charts. We'd sit on the carpet
> and say our sounds.

Asking teachers is not much help, because they mostly can't remember:

> When I was five, I was put in front of the class while the teachers
> added up the registers and told to read to the class . . . I can't
> remember learning to read.

> I can't remember learning to read. I can remember reading to my
> younger brother and saying 'danger' wrong, with a short 'a' and a
> hard 'g'.

> I think I could read before I went to school . . . I can't remember
> anything about it, anyway.

Illustration 24

One teacher, Denise (in her sixties) could remember a little:

> At seven or thereabouts I wasn't reading . . . I'd been to five different schools, messed about during the war . . . education wasn't vital then, it was keeping your children safe and feeding them and worrying about the men away at the war. Then my father sent me to a private school. It was 'cat sat on the mat', Beacon readers, and silence all day from 9 to 3.30. It was run by a tartar of a woman, yes, I know, it was horrendous, I saw that when I became a teacher but I didn't mind it then.

At Tattingstone School, I asked a group of six and seven year olds about how they learned to read:

FS:	Can you tell me this. You people, all of you, I know, can read. Some of you can read better than others 'cos you're older, but all of you can read. I want to know this, I'm going to ask Thomas first. Thomas, how did you learn to read? Who taught you to read? [s] Or did you teach yourself?
Thomas:	***I taught myself.
FS:	How did you teach yourself? [s]
FS:	Do you remember how you first read? [s]
FS:	Do you remember how *you* first read? Justin?
Justin:	I don't know
FS:	Who knows how they first-? Helena.
Helena:	Well the teachers teach us to read and we go home and our mums and dads teach us to read . . . at home.
FS:	Who does the most teaching, the teachers or the mums and dads?
Jesse:	Mums and Dads.
FS:	Why do you think that?
Jesse:	Because at school they don't have enough time to read.
FS:	How did you learn to read, Martha?
Martha:	I don't know.
FS:	You don't know?
	. . .
Daniel:	Well, I forgot now . . . Oh yeh. I think the teachers teach us to read because they read stories sometimes.
FS:	If you never came to school would you learn to read?
All:	No.
FS:	Right. You all think you wouldn't learn to read if you didn't come to school?

[some yesses]

FS: Thomas, you think you would learn to read?

. . .

Thomas: Because my mum and dad might teach me.

FS: You were saying . . . Justin . . . How did your mum and dad teach you to read, Justin?

Justin: Well, how my Mum and Dad taught me to read is they writ words, right, and they said how do you spell 'hear' and I said 'hear', I said 'h' [aspirate], ear, a, r.

FS: [longish monologue on how his son had cards with words and pictures – Mummy, Daddy, car etc.]

Helena: When we did it, mine was like, she got this easy book, my mummy got some of the words out of there to teach me to learn and then she got em a book to read, and it was called, um Green Eggs and Ham *and I still like it.*

FS   [interrupting loudly]: *Green Eggs and Ham, I love it!* [quotes loudly, like an actor] 'I do not like thee Sam-I-am'.

Helena: I still like it [trying to get back into conversation]

FS: That it?

Helena: No. It's 'I am Sam I am Sam Sam I am. Do you like green eggs and ham I do not like them Sam-I-am'.

FS   [still quoting]: 'Do you like them in a boat?'

Helena: No that's not – 'house and mouse'.

The most important aspect of this tape, I'm ashamed to say, is my own prominence. I have been trying for twenty-five years, since I first transcribed my teaching for an Open University BA in Education, to melt into the background, to allow the children to talk, not to dominate the dialogue. Even though to say that our profession gives itself more practice than it allows the children, than it does the learners, is a cliché – I still do it! In lame excuse, I would say that almost all teachers who record their talk with children would have to say the same.

Not only do my words domineer, my tone has a negative effect as well. To Martha, who hasn't spoken yet, I think I am being welcoming, when in fact my voice would put anyone off but a politician determined not to answer a question. I interrupted Helena's happy memories of the Dr Seuss book – I wouldn't like to speculate why. I tell lies without thinking: does ability to read depend on age? Of course not! I embark on long monologues about my family life. Almost all children, on the first day they set foot in a school building, are smarter, more curious, less afraid of what they don't know, better at finding and figuring things out, more confident, resourceful, persistent and independent, than they will ever again be in their school or, unless they are very unusual and lucky, for the rest of their life. This is the view of John Holt, and is quoted in Lang (1988). My conversation with the children is yet another example of children, with all the wit they bring to school, with the clouds of glory still more or less intact, being deprived of language by a teacher.

My account of my behaviour here can stand for almost all other teachers as seen by their students when grown up. Pat jnr remembers being 'stuffed in the deep end'. His mother remembers being 'terrified of the teachers'. Denise remembers 'a tartar of a woman'. Peter's Miss C—— is an exemplary checker, not letting anyone get away with anything, not even an unread 'oh', and Terry's teacher is also a little like a policewoman: 'I'll know if you have, 'cos I'll be asking you about it!' Learning to read, for some, seems to involve frustration, embarrassment and being checked up on. And it involves, if not terror, expected subservience. This was partly because of teachers. But the distress was sometimes due to other factors: the fundamentalism of a family teaching a child to read with the Bible and associated religious leaflets, and the relief the child felt at school, where books were 'normal'. This distress is the first thing that jumps out from the adults and the children talking.

Second, some believe they simply 'catch' reading. Like my son under-standing 'The Red Lion' when he was very young, Ruth, whose parents ran a pub, remembers understanding 'Parker's Ales', and Pat snr believed he was 'born reading'. Peter felt the same: 'I could always read'. For these people, reading is an organic growth that comes, along with speech, with being born and growing through early childhood. Overall, one gets the impression (and this is reinforced by interviews with bilingual children later) that the adults see themselves as children learning about reading at home. By contrast, of course, there were homes with no, or few books, and these people remember reading only at school. Is it not probable that some children who aren't seen to 'catch' reading do in fact do so, but the adults around them are not keen-eyed enough to see it? And is it not also likely that other children not seen to 'catch' reading don't do so because of unhelpful influences from outside them, such as fear and embarrassment, and because of adults taking reading out of the context of life? It is wrong to assume that innate intellectual, perceptual or psychological deficits are always responsible for reading failure.

Then younger people like Terry remember being told to link reading at school with reading at home. This, a crude prototype, perhaps, of Liz Waterland's apprenticeship model, is very different in effect: Terry's teachers were insisting that he got checked on by his parents and they made it clear they would check on him. Waterland, by contrast, is making herself an example of the senior in a reading apprenticeship. She is not policing the learning of reading, but encouraging it by example.

Two final points that can be only flagged here: first, Terry demonstrates that children grow up into adults who remember remarks that teachers made, however trivial those remarks may have been to the teachers at the time. Second, we might note that at least two of my interviewees, when asked about reading, responded in terms of writing. Perhaps my own conviction that the two activities are more related than we as teachers have assumed is a conviction implicit in many children's minds.

Tacolneston's English policy

When I looked at Tacolneston School's English policy, I was struck by the beginning of the part about reading:

> The Literate Child (who leaves our school at 8 years of age) should be able to
>
> * Perceive reading as a life-long activity;
> * Be confident in being able to choose texts through an understanding of, and an ability to express, own likes and dislikes;
> * Know about authors and the 'whole book experience', through intensive school based work with teachers and other adults, as well as authors and illustrators;
> * Use and understand appropriate strategies, for reading fiction and non-fiction, and accessing information;
> * Read in and through a variety of situations, for a variety of purposes, and with different people;
> * Search and think about deeper meanings, both in text and illustration.

What are the emphases here that we might not find in national documents, that emphasise the 'basic skills'? The keywords here are 'life-long', 'likes and dislikes', 'work with . . . authors and illustrators', 'deeper meanings', which are concerned with the realities of being a reader, rather than the banalities of decoding texts. And yet, isn't helping children to see reading as a lifelong activity helping them with a basic skill?

A personal example

My thinking about teaching children to read stems from the fact that I believe that through reading children can imaginatively recreate the world in which they live; that, in combination with thinking and writing, reading has power for change. I want children to become individuals who can lose themselves in a book and experience the unique pleasure that reading can give. I try here to illustrate the power of reading by telling the story of my relationship with a sentence. The pleasure is, I hope, both implicit and obvious in my account. This sentence is translated from the French of Simone Weil (Panichas 1977:46):

Even if our efforts of attention seem for years to be producing no result, one day a light that is in direct proportion to them will flood the soul.

I try, first, to paraphrase, customising the sentence to my life:

All those times I struggled with anything – maths at O level (which I never passed), an apparently impenetrable poem by T. S. Eliot, educational philosophy – every moment of those uncomfortable times that seemed such a waste – well, eventually understanding in exactly fair measure will enlighten my inner being.

My paraphrase is, inevitably, wooden and over-long. But making it enforces my concentration, and makes me reflect to considerable point: on teaching, first. As I watch children struggling with a concept they find difficult, I can now think not just of the benefit to that child for the present or the next ten minutes or so but for the mid- and long-term future. I reflect, second, on Weil's faith: 'in direct proportion'. This affects my behaviour, my way of living, what I do in my work and in my secret, private moments, thinking. The sentence frees me to act in ways that I hadn't thought of before. As I reflect further, the potential of my thought and action widens further. And, as I reflect further still on the sentence, both on my own and in conversation with friends, other sentences and ideas come to mind: Eliot's notion that working on the difficult parts of a poem enables the poem to do its emotional work on the heart, for example. And, further still, that all moments of stilled reflection will one day be distilled in a kind of light.

I could have tried the same exercise with many different sentences. Why does the opening of *Jane Eyre* ('There was no possibility of taking a walk that day') affect me so much? Or the ending of *A Farewell to Arms* ('It was like saying good-bye to a statue. After a while I went out and left the hospital and walked back to the hotel in the rain')? This potential is present in every waking moment of every reading human's life if he or she has been opened up to it. This is as close as I can get, as my deadline approaches and passes, to glimpsing the deeper importance of reading in emphasising and enhancing our humanity.

Closing reading down: easy ways to do it

One can look at the successful teaching of reading by inverting what we want to happen, as Frank Smith (1982) does. How can we make it difficult? Here are some ways (with an accompanying commentary) of closing reading down:

- See children as needing to master rules of reading. (The child may well not understand that such rules exist. They may be of little use anyway.)

- Emphasise phonic skills, despite the huge number of these skills (166, Smith says) and the exceptions. (Do children need phonics to recognise McDonald's? Toys 'R' Us? Their own names? A child who has been read to many times, say *Not Now Bernard* by David McKee, will recognise all the words in it without, necessarily, benefit of phonics.)
- Take letters and words out of context, disregarding the evident fact that children will learn what is meaningful to them, what is in their sphere of reference. (Take *Not Now Bernard* again: the parents with no time for something very important because they have other things to do are in every child's experience. So there is a bridge between this book and all four year olds whether they can read or not.)
- Emphasise word-perfect reading. (Do we insist on our own word-perfect reading of newspapers, advertisements, football and theatre programmes, etc.? If so, we have crippled ourselves.)
- Don't allow guessing. (Adults often guess, hoping – often correctly – that the context will help later on. Notice, especially, how you try to read a newspaper in a language you have some of – but not much. You don't look up each unknown word as you go along. Instead you hope that a later word will shed light on the material.)
- Insist on word-perfect reading. (What is perfect in our lives anyway?)
- Correct all errors immediately. (This teaches the child that reading is a matter of being told you're wrong; nobody likes that. It always discourages learning, and can invoke the 'to hell with it' response. I remember my first driving lesson with some embarrassment. It also removes any sense of meaning from a text if it is constantly being interrupted.)
- Identify and treat problem readers early. (As I have said in my discussion of Reading Recovery (pp. 138ff.), labelling destroys confidence, and is more than likely the main reason for the fact that few adults today are enthusiastic readers.)

Children with English as an additional language

This is the last section I write, and it stands at the edge of my knowledge about children learning to read. I have taught few children who have not possessed English as their first language, but am aware of some of the needs of such children, and some of the richness of their contributions to classrooms. This chapter is in a raw state. I simply wanted the voices of children from different cultures to tell us something about their experiences of reading in England. I do not attempt to answer anything but to sketch the questions these children raise.

Many people all over the world are bilingual because of their circumstances. They grew up in a society, perhaps, that has a residual language still just alive, but they have to speak and write mostly in a dominant language. Some people speak their own tongue and also their oppressors'. Others live near borders of three or four countries, and have to be able to communicate in all the relevant languages. Some countries – Switzerland and Belgium for example (to restrict myself to Europe) – are historically and constitutionally multilingual. Other peoples are educationally multilingual because they have thought it worth the effort to be so. I have mentioned before (p. 78) a pregnant horse I have seen in a cave in Andalusia. The young Spaniard who shows us this horse when we visit Spain addresses the tourists – German, French, English and Spanish – in their own languages.

Britain is unusual. If any nation or people need remedial help, or have special needs, it is the British (among whom I include part of myself) with their ignorance of other languages, and their chauvinistic dismissal of them, and their lazy reluctance to learn them. With their insularity they have been protected from the sheer need that has been, say, Switzerland's. And with their sense of superiority and their imperialism, they have been over proud of their linguistic ignorance. Partly because of this, teachers in the British educational system have, consciously or not, seen bilingualism as a disadvantage. We (the reasoning might go) get by with one language, so it must be terrible to have to cope with two. It doesn't matter if our teaching neglects or even rubs out a first language, as long as the child learns English.

Two French brothers arrived at a school where I was the headteacher. The special needs teacher told me that the mother had 'admitted' that at home, they talked French. The teacher's reaction to this was to wonder how the boys were to be expected to learn English if they were still speaking their first language at home. There are two points here. First, there is the unconscious acceptance that learning English is more important than retaining French. Hundreds of years of colonialist xenophobia are distilled in an unquestioned assumption. Second and more important, as Wiles (1985) says,

> supporting children's first language will not be detrimental to their learning of a second . . . It is language development that is important: the particular language through which this is mediated is less important.

She then quotes research from Bradford (MOTET – Mother Tongue and English Teaching) that showed clearly that

> Punjabi speakers that were taught half the time in Punjabi and half in English in the reception class did better than Punjabi speakers taught full-time in English over the period of a year.

And 'of course', she says, the children taught partly in their own language were 'happier and learned to answer back more rapidly'.

Wiles identifies six considerations in teaching English to children as their second language. First, there is in all of us an innate need to communicate.

Because of this need, bilingual children are highly motivated to learn English, the language of some of the children around them. This echoes something I have written earlier. To see children as essentially in possession of a deficit (here, a language failure) is to see them short. We should see instead their motivation, their will to learn, their innate enthusiasm and sheer love for the world; their passion to relate to that world with, among other things, language. Second, children learning a second language need time listening to that language so that they 'can start to construct their model of that language'. Third, insisting on oral responses too early is counter-productive. Teachers naturally want to see tangible results: this has been a problem in other topics in this book, when, for example, they require unnecessary phonetic correctness in reading, or conventional spelling in writing. But as with those aspects of language, requiring oral responses while children are still building their models of the language, or looking around and making themselves at home in a nursery or a reception class, puts unhelpful pressure on child and teacher alike.

Fourth, children make excellent teachers and helpers. It is all too easy for us to underrate the talk that goes on in the playground. By the same token, children's talk in the classroom (traditionally discouraged by commands and phoney queries like 'Stop talking!' and 'What is going on over there?') is often teaching talk. Or as Wiles writes, 'peer group talk is so important for children's language development'. Again, this a point specially relevant to other parts of my book. Fifth, it is important that bilingual or multilingual children should be fully integrated into the classroom, and take part in all its day-by-day activities. Finally, a new language can't be learnt from a book, but 'untidily with real people in real situations'. Compare this to babies learning to talk. There is no textbook to help them; they use language to learn language.

There are, according to Eve Gregory (1996), several identifiable areas of knowledge that we use when we are reading. The first is *bibliographic*, the knowledge of a culture's story language. As English speakers we might say, while crossing a bridge with a small child, 'Be careful, there might be a troll under this bridge' and expect, rightly, to be understood, to have the joke shared. The same remark with a child whose first language was, for example, Bengali, would not have the same bonding effect, because the Bengali child has inherited a different bibliography, a different set of stories.

This applies in other settings. When we look at reading scheme books, we must bear in mind that children from other cultures come with different knowledge from that assumed by the writers of such schemes. Many children will not know, for example, that English proceeds from left to right; even more will know nothing about the three billy-goats gruff and the troll under the bridge. All this should make us aware of central questions surrounding the issue of teaching bilingual children to read: what experience of books do children bring from home? What English stories are likely to present bilingual children with difficulties? How can we help them to develop a knowledge of a new story language?

Syntactic knowledge is knowledge of the structure of a language. Gregory (1996) says that 'Emergent bilinguals have simply not yet had enough experience in the new language to be familiar with the grammatical structures likely to appear in many early reading books.' *Semantic* knowledge is knowledge of the world. With children used to English as their first language, we can expect them to predict 'chips' after 'fish', 'crackle' and 'pop' after 'snap' in a way that is not possible with children from a different culture, and using a different first language. *Lexical* knowledge, the knowledge of words, is an area in which bilingual children often have a particular strength. Having studied, for example, the Koran without necessarily understanding it, Muslim children have developed an eye for detail. For a full and enlightening discussion of these categories and their relevance to bilingual children, see Gregory's excellent book.

Dawn Sedgwick talked to bilingual children about reading (unpublished research 1997). Shirazul is four years old:

> I see my Mum and Dad and my sisters reading. My Mum reads books, she's got four. She keeps them in the bedroom. The Koran is Arabic. English newspapers come. My brother looks at them sometimes. Not Bengali newspapers. My Dad talk Bengali, but not read. If my Dad got a letter he give it to my Mum to read. My medium size sister go to college. She read there.
>
> I read prayers at the mosque. God helps me. I read some at home. At school I read to my teacher. She points at letters and she say 'What that word is?' If I don't know it I look at the pictures. I learn to read to read books, to read letters. To read at the mosque. Lots of people read at the mosque. They read prayers.

Salma

> My mum reads books with Bengali numbers and pictures. The animals turn into something else in that book. My Dad can read English newspapers but my mum only reads Bengali books. My sisters reads and writes Bengali. She can talk into English and French. I can say hello in French, Bon Jour.
>
> People read magazines at the doctors. Teachers have to read what the children have to do. They have to read letters from the boss about children. My dad at the mosque. He reads Bengali. He says it to God.
>
> My teacher helps me at school. They say, What's that letter? They say the letter to give me a clue. Mrs T—— says 'the' and 'to' and I can. I can write 'we' and 'will' and my sister's name. I learn more

reading at home. I can think better, but I can't think if there's crying and noise and people knocking at the door.

Kitty

My Mum reads Vietnamese newspapers. My sisters reads Chinese books and school books. We have a tray on my sister's bed for special books. I have got a Chinese reading book. I keep it under my covers. I read it when I can't go to sleep. It's got no pictures . . .

At Chinese school we do writing and talk in Chinese. We don't play. I go on Sunday afternoon. At this school, I talk.

Sabina

My Mum and Dad read a book about God. It's Bengali. There are lots of books. A towel is round one book. It is in the drawer. At the mosque a man with a stick reads the Koran. My Dad learned me. That's not Bengali, it's Arabic. Mum and Dad read Bengali newspaper from the Bengali shop . . .

Nobody helped me to read. Just me by myself. My brother learned me. He said 'You try' and I did. He reads a television book to me. Mum and Dad learned at Bangladesh. Their Mum and Dad learned them. You have to learn to read, if you don't you be tell off.

What are these children teaching us? First, they are teaching us about the importance of home, and the importance of religion in many homes. Because much western European culture today is materialistic and agnostic, it may be difficult for us to appreciate the importance of a sacred book. But if we are to understand Muslim children, for example, as potential readers of English, we have to imagine the Koran wrapped and placed in a special position. We have to reconsider in a different light the concept of reading altogether, remembering that many Muslims are still 'people of the Book'.

The children's words suggest that we have to ask whether all homes share the school's policies towards parents. There has always been a gulf between the school's cultural values and the values of the homes that the children come from. As a young teacher I remember my disappointment at the lack of attention that parents paid to my lovingly arranged and yet ultimately pointless displays. When bilingual families are involved, there are further possibilities of breakdown in mutual understanding. For example, Islam forbids the depiction of the human form in art. Thus displays at primary school must be quite alien, or worse, to many Muslim parents. There will be other cultural differences more particularly connected to reading and books.

For mono-lingual children, their work in learning to read is supported by their deep, already practised, knowledge of the spoken language. For children learning to read in an additional language, their already learned spoken language is of less assistance. But note here how Shirazul has taken a phrase from the story of the billy-goats gruff to describe his sister: a mono-lingual child probably would not have done this.

It is worth noticing several aspects of the children's talk that are relevant to all children reading: the way Shirazul, for example, uses context clues ('If I don't know it I look at the pictures'); there is a contrast between settings where the children notice adults reading: the doctor's waiting room on the one hand, and the mosque on the other, and this is related to the fact that there are 'high' purposes for reading (to pray to God, for example, which requires what one child calls 'special' books) and relatively 'low' ones: to pass time in a queue, or to avoid being told off. Salma has noticed how teachers have to read what the boss tells them to do. Whether this is a high or low purpose in her eyes is uncertain. Kitty reinforces an earlier point: she is so strong on detail that, at only five years old, she reads a pictureless book under her covers to help her to go to sleep. Sabina has a view of reading (as Pat snr and Peter do, among the adults) as something organic, something she teaches herself.

Postscript

THE NATIONAL CURRICULUM, AND ONE OFSTED REPORT

Politicians' influence on education has become more and more explicit since the late 1970s. We can glimpse developments in the teaching of English in particular by noting the way in which our elders and betters have changed the name of the subject. The name 'English' was discarded in favour of 'language', because it was more inclusive, and because it acknowledged that teachers of all subjects are teachers of English. Indeed, as late as 1988 a county adviser told me approvingly of a secondary school that had dismantled its English department to make explicit the commitment of all teachers to the subject. Then 'language' disappeared in favour of 'English' with the National Curriculum's subject structure. Now the pronouncements of politicians have brought the word 'literacy' to the fore.

Here I want to bring to the foreground two elements of the political context in which we work as they impinge on my subject.

The National Curriculum: making classroom ceilings transparent

Few of us (teachers, and other workers with children, especially) like to contemplate living outside the law. So the National Curriculum is something we have to live with, or rather under, and, indeed, obey. Many teachers feel that the freakish freedom of the years before and including the 1960s and 1970s, when we taught, more or less, what we liked, was unhealthy. In 1968, obsessed with language, religion and art, I filled the day of my seven year olds with poetry, stories (many of them from the Bible), painting and drawing. I used the school's scheme for mathematics (the ubiquitous Fletcher Mathematics, I think) and *En Avant* for French. I taught no science at all, except for the 'nature study' that grew fitfully out of the walks we took around the school, in the little woods that the new town development had conscientiously left. Other teachers fitted language into a curriculum otherwise based on maths and science. There was, as John White (1990) has said, a need for a national curriculum.

So we have one. There are, though, notorious problems with it that

164

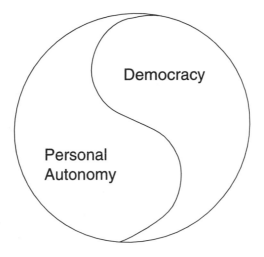

Illustration 25

teachers, nursery nurses, parents and others need to be aware of. The most important is a lack of a moral centre. White (1990) has suggested that this enormous and infinitely serious hole should have had two mutually supporting and conflicting elements: personal autonomy, and life in a democracy (see Illustration 25). To pursue this further, (truth always being more likely to be found in the pursuit of discrepancy) the centre of things might have been found in the line between the two elements, because anyone with total personal autonomy would be unable to survive in a semi-democratic society. Or that society would not survive. White puts it like this:

> it made good sense to think of the child's well-being both as embracing a concern for others' flourishing and as premised on a self-determined life.

Instead of a creative friction between these two notions, what was imposed on the nation's teachers and children was an atomistic and management-led syllabus that effectively changed the working definition of the word accountable from 'responsible professionally to our children and our colleagues' to 'responsible to politicians', who then used the curriculum and the rest of the so-called 'reform' apparatus to made the ceilings of classroom transparent. The marginalisation of the arts was, once the lack of a moral centre became clear, inevitable, because the arts constantly challenge moral and social assumptions. This marginalisation in language can be seen most clearly in the low frequency and importance of the word 'poetry' compared to 'spelling', 'handwriting' and 'punctuation'. Language largely stopped being its substantive issue, communication with oneself and others, and became its periphery, presentation.

165

The second problem with the National Curriculum is the accretion of administrative tasks for teachers that are nothing to do with education. If the classroom's ceiling is now transparent, so are teachers' living rooms, or wherever they do their preparation. It matters as much now to our managers whether we have done all our checklisting and short-, mid- and long-term planning, as whether we are efficient and inspirational in the classroom. We need to know now what level a child is on, before we can think about his or her passions and capabilities. Politicians control teachers to an extent neither politicians nor teachers would have believed possible a generation ago. Teachers ceased being what they had been, at least to some extent, for most of a century – creative individuals with various qualities – and became little more than hired hands implementing, first a curriculum, and later, a way of teaching a curriculum imposed on them by non-professionals determined to please the supposed prejudices of middle England.

Like Margaret Browne and her colleagues at Tacolneston, we can offer children more than the lowest common denominator that the National Curriculum insists on: for example, consistent punctuation, regular handwriting and so on. Perhaps the gap between what the National Curriuculum aims at and what children can achieve can be glimpsed in its sentence about organising writing, where the writers move from the 'cumulative pattern of a poem' to the 'ingredients for a cake'.

An OFSTED report

What does an OFSTED report mean to a school, especially as far as language is concerned? Margaret Browne of Tacolneston sent me her report early in January 1998. I described this school in my introduction and I have referred to it throughout. I wanted to see how it would fare in an evaluation. Margaret had already told me roughly what it said: outstanding. What follows is as much a critique of OFSTED's methods as it is of Tacolneston.

> Talconeston . . . is an outstanding school at the heart of the village community. It provides a rich and stimulating education which gives [the children] clear insights into the world beyond their small school . . . Excellent provision is made for children's personal development, and the quality of the teaching is consistently very good. Children are very well behaved and endlessly enthusiastic . . . in speaking and listening and writing, children make good progress throughout the school, and most reach national expectations by the age of seven, with a significant minority doing better . . . in reading . . . the majority exceed national norms by the age of seven. Even the youngest children listen carefully and respectfully to their teachers.

166

Imagine here a voice fading out. The voice has been talking for so long that we know by now what it is going to say. We have certainly got the tone right: bland as custard, patronising. It spoke to us from the middle and last years of the Tory government, and it speaks to us now, in the early years of the Labour one.

We have also got a message: this is a good school. I am encouraged here, because the Woodhead[1] message of the past few years might have led me to expect a less positive response. Whenever I despair, I think of the imaginations and enthusiasms of these inspectors that were not dampened by their employers. But suddenly I hit a sentence that I read four times: 'Sometimes, their progress with the skills of spelling and punctuation lag behind their facility with words.' It should, of course, have been 'lags'. More to the point this is a commonplace: any child with verbal facility will outstrip his or her skills in punctuation and spelling. But, even more importantly: why couldn't that sentence have been written the other way round? I tried it out: 'Their facility with words outstrips their skills in spelling and punctuation.'

Here is another voice fading out, mine. For none of us knows everything. All party-political confidence is false. Someone said recently of a film director that he never finished a film, he had it taken away from him. Similarly, Paul Valéry said of a poem that it 'is never finished, only abandoned'. My book is like that; a temporary stay against my confusion about education, language and the times we live in. It is about the difference between, on the one hand, education pundits who are sure of children as owners, in school terms, only of deficits and faults and failings; as children who are in need of 'remedial' help, who are labelled as 'special needs' children; and thinkers, on the other hand, who see children as comets trailing clouds of glory. Alastair, George, Justin, Daniel, Helena, Thomas, Jesse, Jo-Anne, Matthew, Jerlisa and Leisha and my other correspondents, Shirazul, Salma, Kitty . . . and all the others speak for this view. They surprise and transcend objectives, targets and checklists. These comets trailing clouds of glory are owners of abilities and strengths that we as adults (in spite of everything governments throw at us, we still have a choice) can either neglect or nourish.

---

1 Chris Woodhead is Chief Inspector of Schools.

REFERENCES

I have not included references to the Bible, novels by Jane Austen and James Joyce, the plays of Shakespeare, the poems of Wordsworth, Dickinson, Larkin, Blake and other pillars of our civilisation. Neither (for different reasons) have I referenced ephemera such as letters to newspapers. Other unreferenced quotations – for example, from the works of Robert Frost and Seamus Heaney – are unreferenced partly because I have lost the sources, and partly because they too are, in my world, pillars of our civilisation.

Agard, John and Nichols, Grace (1991) *No Hickory No Dickory No Dock: A Collection of Caribbean Nursery Rhymes*. London, Viking

Barrs, Myra (1987) 'Mapping the world', *English in Education* 21:1.

Bearne, Eve (ed.) (1995) *Greater Expectations: Children Reading Writing*. London, Cassell.

Browne, Ann (1993) *Helping Children to Write*. London, Paul Chapman.

Burgess, Anthony (1992) *A Mouthful of Air: Language and Languages, Especially English*. London, Hutchinson.

Cashdan, A., Esland, G. M., Grugeon, E., Harris, A. E., *et al.* (1972) *Language in Education: A Source Book*. London, Routledge and Kegan Paul with Open University Press.

Causley, Charles (1974) *The Puffin Book of Magic Verse*. London, Puffin.

Causley, Charles (1996) *Collected Poems for Children*. London, Macmillan.

Chomsky, Noam (1972) 'Language and the mind', in A. Cashdan *et al.*, *Language in Education: A Source Book*. London, Routledge and Kegan Paul with Open University Press.

Czerniewska, Pat (1992) *Learning about Writing: The Early Years*. Oxford, Blackwell.

Daniels, Harry (1993) 'Perspectives on reading difficulty', in M. Styles and M.J. Drummond (eds) *The Politics of Reading*. University of Cambridge Institute of Education and Homerton College.

Dombey, Henrietta (1992) Article in *English in Education* 26.

Dowker, Ann (1996) 'Discovering the poetry of the preschool child', *Montessori Education* 7:5.

Drummond, Mary Jane (1993) *Assessing Children's Learning*. London, David Fulton.

Drummond, Mary Jane (1998) 'Children yesterday, today and tomorrow', in C. Richards and P. Taylor (eds) *How Shall We School our Children?* London, Falmer.

Fox, Carol (1993) *At the Very Edge of the Forest*. London, Cassell.

Goodman, Kenneth S. (1982) *Language and Literary*, 2 vols. London, Routledge and Kegan Paul.

Graves, Donald (1983) *Writing: Teachers and Children at Work*. London, Heinemann.

Gregory, Eve (1996) *Making Sense of a New World: Learning to Read in a Second Language*. London, Paul Chapman.

Grugeon, Elizabeth (1988) 'Underground knowledge: what the Opies missed', *English in Education* 22:2.

Hallworth, Grace (1994) *Buy a Penny Ginger and Other Rhymes*. London, Longman.

Heaney, Seamus and Hughes, Ted (1982) *The Rattle Bag: An Anthology of Poetry*. London, Faber and Faber.

Hughes, Martin (1989) 'The Child as learner: the contrasting views of developmental psychology and early education', in C. Desforges (ed.) *Early Childhood Education*, British Journal of Educational Psychology Monograph 4. Scottish Academic Press.

Jean, Georges (1987) *Writing: The Story of Alphabets and Scripts*. London, Thames and Hudson, 1992.

Lang, Peter (ed.) (1988) *Thinking about Personal and Social Education in the Primary School*. Oxford, Blackwell.

Lurie, Alison (1990) *Don't Tell the Grown-Ups: Subversive Children's Literature*. London, Bloomsbury.

Opie, Iona and Opie, Peter (1959) *The Lore and Language of Schoolchildren*. Oxford, Oxford University Press.

Opie, Iona and Opie, Peter (1988) *The Singing Game*. Oxford, Oxford University Press.

Panichas, George (ed.) (1977) *The Simone Weil Reader*. New York, Mackay.

Pollard, Andrew and Tann, Sarah (1993) *Reflective Teaching in the Primary School*. London, Cassell.

Robinson, Anne, Crawford, Leslie and Hall, Nigel (1990) *Some Day You Will No All About Me: Young Children's Explorations in the World of Letters*. London, Mary Glasgow.

Rosen, Michael and Steele, Susanna (1990) *Inky Pinky Ponky: Collected Playground Rhymes*. London, Collins.

Sedgwick, Dawn and Sedgwick, Fred (1993) *Drawing to Learn*. London, Hodder and Stoughton.

Sedgwick, Dawn and Sedgwick, Fred (1996) *Learning Together: Enhance Your Child's Creativity*. London, Bloomsbury.

Sedgwick, Fred (1991) *Lies*. Liverpool, Headland.

Sedgwick, Fred (1993) *The Expressive Arts*. London, David Fulton.

Sedgwick, Fred (1994) *Pizza, Curry, Fish and Chips*. London, Longman.

Sedgwick, Fred (1997a) *Read My Mind: Young Children, Poetry and Language*. London, Routledge.

Sedgwick, Fred (1997b) *Blind Date*. Ipswich, Tricky Sam!

Sedgwick, Fred (1997c) 'Dear Jerlisa, Dear Leisha: young children writing letters', *Montessori Education* 8: 4.

Sedgwick, Fred (1998) 'Nil on Entry', *Montessori Education*.

Shaw, Frank (1970) *You Know Me Anty Nelly? Liverpool Children's Rhymes*. London, Wolfe.

Smith, Frank (1982) *Writing and the Writer*. London, Heinemann.

Spiegelman, Art (1987) *Maus: A Survivor's Tale*. Harmondsworth, Penguin.

Styles, Morag and Drummond, Mary Jane (eds) (1993) *The Politics of Reading*. University of Cambridge Institute of Education and Homerton College.

Summerfield, Geoffrey (1970) *Junior Voices: The First Book*. Harmondsworth, Penguin.

Tizard, Barbara and Hughes, Martin (1984) *Young Children Learning: Talking and Thinking at Home and at School*. London, Fontana.

Valencia, Robert (1997) *The Evolution of Deficit Thinking: Educational Thought and Practice*. London, Falmer.

Vernon, P. E. (ed.) (1970) *Creativity: Selected Readings*. Harmondsworth, Penguin.

Walkerdine, Valerie and Lucey, Helen (1989) *Democracy in the Kitchen*. London, Virago.

Walter, Colin (1989) *An Early Start to Poetry*. London, Macdonald.

Waterland, Liz (1986) *Read With Me*. Stroud, Thimble Press.

Waterland, Liz (1998) *The Read with Me Handbook*. Stroud, Thimble Press.

Watson, Victor (1993) 'Multi-layered texts and multi-layered readers', in M. Styles and M. J. Drummond (eds) *The Politics of Reading*. University of Cambridge Institute of Education and Homerton College.

Wells, Gordon (1986) *The Meaning Makers: Children Learning Language and Using Language to Learn*. London, Hodder and Stoughton.

Wells, Gordon and Nicholls, John (eds) (1985) *Language and Learning: An Interactional Perspective*. London, Falmer.

Whitehead, Marian (1993) 'Born again phonics and the nursery rhyme revival', *English in Education* 27:3.

White, John (1990) *Education and the Good Life: Beyond the National Curriculum*. London, Kogan Page.

Wiles, Silvaine (1985) 'Language and learning in multiethnic classrooms: strategies for supporting bilingual students', in G. Wells and J. Nicholls (eds) *Language and Learning: An Interactional Perspective*. London, Falmer.

Wilkinson, Andrew (1989) 'Our first great conversationalists', *English in Education* 23:2.

INDEX